BRIDE-MADE

BRIDE-MADE

A Memoir

MIA J. HANKS

Mia J. Hanks

To my parents,
My greatest supporters.
- Your favorite daughter

To my children,
My pride, my joy, and my inspiration.
- Mom

To Stitch,
You'll always be my 'ohana.
- Lilo

Prologue

I was first approached with the idea of writing a book about narcissistic abuse a year after I walked away from my 29 year marriage. A book sounded like a monumental task. I was not a writer. My writing experience was limited to a couple of English classes in college. Nonetheless, I began jotting down notes and making lists of the stories that I would tell if I ever did decide to write. Those scribbles of notes worked their way into an outline, and that outline became a series of vignettes. Before I knew it I had something that somewhat resembled a book. My hope is that this collection of stories and experiences can be helpful to others out there who might be living in situations like the one I lived in for so many years- Abusive situations that are not obvious to the outside world. Vulnerability is not my strongest point, but if my candidness can help even one person, then it is worth it to me. Narcissistic abuse is all too real and too prevalent in our society. Lives are being damaged every day. This hidden abuse cannot remain hidden. It's time to speak. This is my story.

"*There is nothing more confining than the prison we don't know we are in.*"

- Shakespeare

I

The Beginning

At the age of 19 I fell for a narcissist. I was young, naive and in my first year of college, far from home for the very first time. Coming from a small rural community, the bright lights of the big city offered a new perspective for me. I quickly and excitedly began adapting to my new home away from home, enjoying my new friends and the novelty that comes with being a college freshman A few months into this new college experience I agreed to a double date, a blind date actually. And that's when I met him. An evening on the town and a nice dinner followed by a movie made for a successful first meeting. My date seemed like the perfect guy. He was nice, smart and came from a wealthy family so he had opportunities everywhere. And he was seemingly enamored by me, as he made no delays in calling me after our first encounter. I was initially unsure what to think of him, but I was certainly intrigued. How could all the attention that he was pouring onto me be a bad thing? He was falling in love with me, I was sure of it, especially when he secretly obtained a copy of my class schedule from the registrar's office just so he could adjust his daily routes to seemingly bump into me. Stalking? Maybe. But to a 19 year-old naive college student it seemed that I was the center of his universe.

All the gifts, the attention, nothing went unnoticed. He took me to nice dinners and planned our dates down to the finest detail. Our first official date was no exception. He arranged to have his roommate dress up as a flower vendor. This young man patiently waited on the city's riverwalk until we came strolling by after an Italian dinner, and my date, right on cue, purchased ALL of the roses his roommate was "selling." Unbeknownst to me, my newfound admirer called his mother after this first date and informed her that he had met the girl he would marry. In the following months I was showered with cards, flowers and small gifts, always to the amazement of my friends. He loved to make statements with his grand displays of love, and my friends were duly impressed. He was the boyfriend they all wished they had. His attentiveness to me was obvious, even to the casual observer. This young man seemed almost too good to be true.

A few months into our dating relationship my boyfriend presented me with his fraternity pin. In collegiate Greek life this was a serious pledge, a precursor to engagement. I proudly wore his pin on a gold chain as a necklace and I couldn't have been happier. However, according to my peer group, it seemed a bit fast. None of them had received pins, but then again we were the exceptional couple. We were bound for the altar, and no one would disagree with that. About a year later I would in fact add an engagement ring to my gift collection, and by the time I was 21 we were married. What I had failed to realize during our courtship was that it had all been glamor, smoke and mirrors. I had not been courted. I had been acquired.

After marriage it did not take me long to realize that I was no longer the center of my husband's universe Instead, I existed to serve him. I started to notice that while he loved to have fun, it was only fun if it was on his terms and schedule. That was okay with me. I was eager to be a good and supportive wife. When things didn't go his way or I failed to meet his expectations, he would pout like a spoiled child for long periods of time until I took the blame for whatever circumstance that had gone against his plans. Once I took the responsibility for our problems, it was like nothing ever happened. All I had to do was accept the blame, no matter what. In these early days I considered this to be an adjustment period. We were learning to cohabitate and I was sure it must be normal for things to not start out perfectly. I was happy enough, and I was determined to make this marriage work. As a result, I willingly settled into a daily routine of power imbalances.

If I chose to stand up for myself and my decisions I was given the silent treatment. It was my husband's weapon of choice; to treat me like I didn't exist. I hated being invisible in my own marriage, but this is how it was until I conceded to his authority. I learned early on in marriage that it was better to comply and keep the peace, to keep my opinions to myself, to treat his accomplishments as if he was the greatest man alive and to make him my number one priority. As long as I served his whims and wishes, I was "allowed" to be the love of his life. I was being slowly groomed into a compliant victim. I became a prisoner in a golden cage and I wasn't even aware that I was helping to build it.

2

Diet Coke

Fast forward 25 years. I am on my hands and knees in our master bathroom cleaning up a huge mess. I was married with two teenage children and I was living in a big, beautiful home in the suburbs. I had everything I could ever want; a maid, a gardener, private schools for the kids and nice cars. To the outside world I had it all. I was living the perfect dream. But on this particular day the "dream"was a nightmare. I was sitting on the cold tiles of the floor, cleaning a mess that I had apparently created. A large styrofoam cup full of ice and diet coke had just been hurled all over our elegant master bathroom. The ice cubes had hit the shower glass with a shattering loud pop, and diet coke covered the floor, the bathtub and my vanity mirror. It was a sight to witness as it went sloshing through the air, looking like a glowing thundercloud of mindless rage. And it was I who was left to clean up the sticky residue of this tantrum.

The event leading up to this pageantry had been my fault, as usual. My husband needed to talk to me about upcoming plans for the day. There was not a look on his face that anything was amiss as he stood there casually drinking his diet coke. We were in the middle of our discussion when my teenage daughter entered the room and asked me to help her with her hair. I thought nothing of this quick diversion, and took a hairbrush to assist her. "Hang on," I said to my husband, "We can finish this conversation in a few minutes." And it just so happened that when I had finished with that five minute hair task, the phone rang. I spent the next two minutes on the phone rescheduling an appointment. A few minutes of my time re-channeled to handling menial tasks. It didn't seem like a cataclysm to me, but apparently it did to my husband. Without warning, the diet coke went flying through the air. This act of neglecting his needs, as he saw it, angered my husband to the point of throwing a fit worthy of a cranky toddler. This five or six minutes that I "wasted," according to him, should have been spent on time with him, hearing about the important things he wanted to discuss at that very moment.

Patience was not my husband's forte. When he wanted something, he didn't and wouldn't wait. How dare I focus my attention on the mundane tasks of family and home when he needed my undivided attention. Nothing should ever come before him, and the random interruptions of everyday life were not tolerated. No one impedes or defies the king, and especially not in his kingdom. If he wanted to talk to me or needed me and I needed to take a quick phone call or help my kids, it wasn't acceptable. Everyone and everything should take a backseat to him; kids, pets, phone calls, you name it. He was the absolute master of his castle. At least this is what he perceived. He was the CEO, the boss, the god. So, to make his point clear, he threw his diet coke all over the bathroom and stormed out, slamming the door and making a scene as he always did to assert his authority. Intimidation by making a "splash" was his strong suit, and I spent the next 20 minutes cleaning up his splash.

My husband wasn't sorry, and he didn't think he had acted erratically. His behavior was, in fact, completely appropriate given the injustice that had just been served to him by his ungrateful and inattentive wife. He had been disrespected and wronged to his face by this woman who dared to put anyone but him first above all. He was more than just angry, he was furious. Not because of a hairbrush and a phone call, but because his reality, his universe, had been put on the most infinitesimal of holds. It sounds trivial to a rational person, but not to my narcissistic husband. Once again, a perfectly good day had been so quickly ruined in an instant. Repercussions would soon follow, as they always did, for upsetting his entire world.

My husband's silent treatment would last for hours or days or maybe a week. He would ignore me, literally as if I was invisible, to make his point. I would become depressed because I was being ostracized by the man who claimed to love me, until I made things right and apologized. He comes first always. His needs are the greatest, and his tantrums were extremely effective at crumbling what little self esteem and identity I had as a woman, mother and wife. So I cleaned up his mess. I wanted to make this incident disappear so we could continue on with our day and I could be a person again and treated as more than a forgotten ghost in my own home. I thought the faster I could clean up the mess, the faster the problem could vanish, and maybe, just maybe, he would forget about being angry with me. It was wishful thinking. He would be angry for an absurd amount of time. My faults were always at the forefront of his mind, so that his anger at me would be justified and well deserved. Should I have refused this cleaning task? Should I have left the coke residue all over the bathroom until he agreed to clean it up? In retrospect, probably. Hindsight is always 20/20. However, I didn't refuse. At the time I still thought I was the problem. If I had just been a better wife, listened more, put him first...I was still caught in the golden trap and after 25 years of marriage, I was well versed in cleaning up his messes to make our life appear normal to the outside world. But it was a false normal. It was a lie. And I did everything I could to keep up that lie, even lying to myself.

3

Books and Highlighters

One thing to know about narcissists is they love to teach, especially to those they see as "servants." In their mind they are the smartest people in the room, even when in reality they're not. I had many faults, according to my husband. He said all my faults revolved around my prioritizations and how I managed my time. He felt that I placed everyone and everything ahead of him. Our children, any crisis that came up, everyday tasks that had to be done, any responsibilities that I or others had, even life itself were not "allowed" to be more important than him. My inattentiveness was unfathomable to him, and it was the source of nearly every fight we'd had over the past 28 years of marriage. So, in true narcissistic fashion, he decided that I needed to be fixed so that I could better serve him. He had had enough of my disrespect and imperfection.

I required fixing, and my husband was up to the task. He was smart, wealthy and all powerful. He deserved everything he wanted. He could buy anything he wanted. He deserved and demanded perfection. He had never been happy in our 28 years of marriage, not once, or so he had said in yet another fit of rage. So he developed a plan to fix his imperfect wife. He began purchasing books; books about marriage and how to prioritize your spouse. He got books on how to restore intimacy and improve connection with your husband. He found books on how to make your spouse happy and how to strengthen your marriage. It might sound like a reasonable plan, but he was not a reasonable man. In his infamous condescending form he presented a stack of books to me one evening, about 8 in total. "I bought these for you." Oh wow, a gift. But it certainly was not the kind of gift I wanted. This was an iron fist hidden in a velvet glove. Still, I graciously accepted. After all, he had spent time researching to find the best books on how to "rehabilitate" me. I, his disappointment of a wife, should be grateful, or so he believed.

He explained his detailed plan to me. He wanted me to read these books in the order he had chosen, and he wanted me to learn from this literature. He explained that these books would help me become the wife he wanted me to be: complacent, compliant and submissive. Apparently they would be a miracle cure for our marriage. He wanted to make sure I read his stack of books that he had so lovingly purchased. What a great husband he was to honor me with such a gift. So he handed me high-lighters- several highlighters in all different colors. I was to read, study and highlight. Those were my instructions. My husband stressed the use of the highlighters. "Highlight things that are interesting and then we can discuss the highlighted sections together after you finish each section of the book." Would there be a quiz over the material when I finished? Absolutely, without question. He had to make sure I had actually read the book. He was going to force a connection with me if it was the last thing he did.

Did I actually read this cluster of books? Not really. I retreated to my reading nook each evening and enjoyed a little bit of peace and quiet while I flipped through these books. I found that it was easy to highlight random sections, making it look like I had really been doing my homework. I carefully highlighted different parts in different colors. I made it look like I was color coding each book. After all, I knew my husband would check these books to see that I had been using the highlighters appropriately. And for good measure I even dog eared pages to make the books look more worn and used. He had to believe that his plan was working. Actually, I was reading the table of contents and skimming through the "interesting parts" so that I would have some talking points when he held our discussion sessions.

Instead, however, I used this alone time to research relationship problems. Something had to be wrong. I was 49 years old, sitting like a naive student amongst a stack of relationship self-help books, presumably teaching me how to be a better wife. And don't forget the assortment of highlighters too. This could not be normal. It was becoming clear to me, after 28 years of marriage, that most people don't live like this. At least I didn't know anyone who seemed to be living this way. Most people couldn't sanely survive like this. What was I doing, and how was I continuing to persevere in this environment? I had to find out what was happening to me because whatever it was, it was getting worse by the day.

I took out my laptop and began Googling words like "toxic" and "emotional abuse." I found online quizzes with titles like "Are You Being Emotionally Abused?" and "Is Your Relationship Toxic?" I took every quiz I could find on the internet. I lost count of how many I took, but all the results were unnerving. My quiz score would almost always put me in the "Severe Abuse" category, followed by information on how to get help. Usually a phone number to the domestic abuse hotline would be included in these results. Also, resources for how to find help, women's shelters, and so on. Surely my life wasn't this bad? Was I answering the questions on the quizzes accurately? I knew something was wrong, but there was just no way this could be me. I couldn't be an abuse victim. And then I happened upon an Instagram post one night while I was scrolling through social media that was a game changer. It was a simple quote, but it changed my perspective in an instant.

"True intimacy isn't about sex. It is about being able to look at your partner and say, 'I feel safe with you'."

Did I feel safe? I had never asked myself this question. So I did. Do I feel safe? No, absolutely not. Not for one second. I felt unsafe, unstable, un-content, and unhappy. I took more quizzes and did more online reading. I researched and read what healthy relationships looked like, and I found the same basic list of traits across many different internet sites.

The freedom to have open and honest communication
A feeling of safety in the relationship
An ability to be vulnerable
A sense of trust
Both partners being accountable for their actions
A sense of connection
Unconditional support

I found I had none of these things in my marriage. The realization was as humbling to me as it was shocking. I was a victim of abuse, and I had helped put myself there with my compliance and my naiveté. My desire to be a good wife had been my husband's best weapon against me. I came to the conclusion that my relationship wasn't healthy. Not even remotely healthy. None of these traits that I read about were present in my marriage. Instead, the "unhealthy traits" painted a much more accurate portrait of my life.

Poor communication
Disrespect
Emotional abuse
Lack of trust

Criticism and ridicule
Passive aggressive behavior
A lack of emotional support

I was using my "book time" wisely. While my husband thought I was learning to be a better, more submissive wife with multi-colored highlighters in hand, I was actually beginning to learn that I was an abused wife. The pieces to the puzzle were finally beginning to fit together. A new picture was emerging and it was frightening. I did more internet research. I had to know more. Was I really an abuse victim? This seemed crazy but logical all at the same time. With research and more reading I stumbled upon the final piece to the puzzle that had plagued me for so long. I had the answer to the question of why I was so unhappy and why my family and my life felt so dysfunctional. These two words that I had discovered would change my life forever. Covert Narcissism.

I had secretly thought of my husband as a narcissist for years, but not overtly. He wasn't necessarily showy. He was a "nice, humble guy." No one would ever believe me to be an abuse victim. I had the perfect husband after all. But then I learned about covert narcissism. I never knew such a variant of narcissism existed. This was a secretive, vulnerable type of narcissism. Hidden mental and psychological abuse. The white collar crime of domestic violence. Bingo. My husband was a textbook case of covert narcissism right here, in real life, living in my house, controlling every aspect of me, forcing me to be another tool in the machine that was his happiness and his universe, and no one knew but me...

Narcissistic Criteria

The Diagnostic and Statistical Manual of Mental Disorders (DSM-5) describes Narcissistic Personality Disorder as possessing at least five of the following nine criteria.

Has a grandiose sense of self-importance (e.g. - exaggerates achievements and talents, expects to be recognized as superior without commensurate achievements)

Is preoccupied with fantasies of unlimited success, power, brilliance, beauty, or ideal love

Believes that he or she is "special" and unique and can only be understood by, or should associate with, other special or high-status people (or institutions)

Requires excessive admiration

Has a sense of entitlement (i.e. - unreasonable expectations of especially favorable treatment or automatic compliance with his or her expectations)

Is interpersonally exploitative (i.e. - takes advantage of others to achieve his or her own ends)

Lacks empathy: is unwilling to recognize or identify with the feelings and needs of others

Is often envious of others or believes that others are envious of him or her

Shows arrogant, haughty behaviors or attitudes.

4

Covert Narcissism

In a nutshell, narcissists live for themselves. It's all about them all the time. While everyone may have some narcissistic tendencies, Narcissistic Personality Disorder is another beast altogether. It's not just traits or tendencies, it's a way of life. A complete personality. A personality disorder, emphasis on the word disorder. Narcissistic Personality Disorder requires at least five of the nine traits previously listed, and my husband had a clear nine traits, maybe ten. There was no doubt. He was and is a textbook case. Discovering this "diagnosis," even though it wasn't a formal one, was life changing for me. I finally understood what had been going on in my marriage and why life had been unbearable for so many years. Reading this list of NPD traits, I felt like someone must have lifted the roof on our house and peered inside. This list described my husband perfectly.

He wasn't simply a "narcissist." He had Narcissistic Personality Disorder.

Narcissists feel as though they are more important than the "average" person and therefore they require more and more and more. More admiration, more attention, more sympathy, more praise, and on and on and on. Overt narcissists are just that-overt. They are showy, flamboyant and outwardly arrogant. This is the personality type that is generally attributed to the word narcissist. The covert narcissists, however, present a bit differently. While the DSM criteria still captures their essence, they are more secretive with their traits. Instead of outward arrogance, they prefer to play the victim and gain sympathy. They want attention, positive or negative, but the covert narcissist's favorite kind of attention might just be sympathy. Sympathy for their victimhood. A covert narcissist is almost always a victim in their own mind. It's impossible to treat them good enough. There is a piece of them that always seems to be victimized, making them most deserving of all their wants and wishes. My husband was a victim at his core, and it was almost impossible to grant him the amount of attention that he felt he deserved.

While they are excessively entitled, just as the DSM describes, covert narcissists will tuck this entitlement trait away and make it their job to appear humble and kind. Will they take advantage of others for their own gain? Absolutely. But they will do it in a sneaky fashion where it's not obvious to the casual observer. My husband was the definition of "entitled" during our marriage. He was more deserving of good deeds than anyone else in the house. He worked harder, he made the most money, he was the smartest and he truly believed he was the most deserving. Only the best was good enough for him. However, he didn't act entitled outside our home. He acted humble, and no one outside of our family knew the depths of his entitlement. He wore his mask of humility proudly and he was convincing.

Narcissists want their achievements praised to the highest degree, yet they may appear humble despite the praise. My husband wanted credit and praise for everything he did, even the smallest act. On a particularly busy day when I was shuffling the kids around I asked him to take the dog to a quick vet appointment. It was just for a vaccine; not a big deal. He agreed to this task and I was thankful that he could help me out. For the next couple of days after this random act of kindness, my husband wanted credit. He wanted to be praised for his act of service. He reminded me multiple times that he had taken the dog to the vet, just in case I might have forgotten. He was such a good husband. So helpful. In his opinion he had gone above and beyond. Surely no other husband ever helped out like he did. He wanted praise. And more praise. This shouldn't have been a big deal, but to him it was. We should loudly proclaim his kindness, his achievements, and all of his good deeds to the highest degree. This was expected.

Narcissists live with the grand fantasies of an ideal life. Ideal love, ideal success. Nothing is ever quite good enough for them. And while you may believe them to be unostentatious, try as you might you can't ever please a narcissist, for their ideals are not humanly attainable. I was never enough for my husband. Nothing was ever good enough. I might be close to enough, but he always let me know that I never quite made the mark. The problem was that nothing would ever meet his expectations. He always seemed to expect perfection and it wasn't reachable. Nearly everything I did was critiqued. My husband thought he was being helpful by helping me to improve. He wanted to help me be more organized, a better driver, a better cook, an all around better wife, and so on down the line. Everything I did was met with criticism, but in his mind I should be grateful for his attentiveness to detail. After all, he was helping me improve myself. I didn't need self help books. I had a narcissistic husband.

Overt narcissists stand out in a crowd. Yet covert narcissists are harder to spot. They are sneaky and sly, manipulative and conniving. Covert narcissists are considered the most dangerous types of narcissists for this very reason. They are chameleons, adjusting their colors to their environment. They hide in plain sight. Everyone around us believed my husband to be a nice guy, both kind and charming. No one would ever believe that he was anything but a fine and decent husband, but behind closed doors his charm was a trap. Falling into a trap with a covert narcissist is a slippery slope and so much easier than one might think. I had fallen down that slippery slope at 19 years old, and getting up again after 30 years would be the hardest obstacle I would ever encounter.

5

The Newlywed Game

So let's rewind...Narcissistic abuse is insidious, and it's harder to detect when you're dealing with a covert narcissist. Especially when you're young, naive, 21 years old and newly married. Covert narcissists are covert. In public they have a persona to uphold, but it's all an act. My narcissistic husband and I looked like the perfect couple. We were fresh out of college, new home owners and setting up a life together in a small west Texas town. Life should have been good, and it was sometimes. But no one would ever suspect what was going on behind closed doors. Narcissists like my husband have a need for constant control. Constant attention. Constant praise. As a young adult I saw friends and family praising my husband. What a wonderful young man he is. So smart, so successful and such an attentive spouse. I was outnumbered. Surely all of these people couldn't be wrong? Surely it must just be me who saw him as controlling and manipulating, and my perception must be flawed. This became my mindset for years and years. And I stayed in this marriage year after year after year. The more I forgave and reconciled with his behavior, the worse the abuse got. I became a voluntary victim, and before I knew it I was in over my head. This was the life I had landed in, and even though it didn't feel completely right, I needed to make it work. I couldn't walk away and risk disappointing both my family and his. In my mind I had no other choice but to master the art of surviving under my husband's micromanagement.

I learned to think five steps ahead and I always tried to anticipate his mood. His mood could change with the wind, and I wanted to be ready and able to anticipate these changes. If he needed a drink of water, I learned to jump up and retrieve it. If he needed an errand run, I happily did it. And when I was nine months pregnant, he wouldn't hesitate to ask me to run upstairs and retrieve his briefcase, or whatever it was that he needed at the moment. He showed little to no compassion for me, and I allowed this neglect. I rarely, if ever, confronted him, and if I did I was met with the same response- "You're just being too sensitive." My goal was to keep him happy so that our lives could run smoothly. His needs came before mine or anyone else's. He was the king of his castle, and he was my full time job. That's just how he wanted it, and he was the absolute worst boss.   I was at his beck and call 24/7, and if I wasn't he gave me the silent treatment; sometimes for days, maybe weeks. Life had to revolve around him at all times. His happiness was of paramount concern. If he wasn't happy, no one was allowed to be happy, and that's how we rolled. He had an insatiable need to be entertained, and when he was happy, life was good. We were financially successful and we enjoyed the fruits of our labors. Nice trips, fun adventures and lots of laughs. It was good until it wasn't. And since every day wasn't bad, since there were good days too, it must not be abuse, or so I thought. I later would learn that this is referred to as "bread crumbing," and my husband dropped a lot of breadcrumbs, always at just the right intervals.

Bread crumbing is an all too common technique used in many toxic relationships. The victim is given just enough attention, time and affection to keep them hooked, but never enough to meet their emotional needs. Just enough good days interspersed amongst the bad days. Bread crumbs. And so the victim remains a victim, waiting for the next good day or good deed to happen. Behavior from an abuser is cyclical with highs and lows, and with the highs come bread crumbs. A small but inconsistent supply of interest. Over time, bread crumbing can lead the victim to lower their standards. We victims convince ourselves to start expecting just the bare minimum. The bare minimum of goods days, of pleasant behavior, or adequate treatment from the narcissist. This keeps the narcissist in a position of control- their favorite place to be.

I learned to live for the "bread crumb" moments. And when life was good for a couple of weeks I knew the bad would be coming soon. I was ready for it. I began to expect his behavior to deteriorate around holidays. This was likely due to the fact that the busiest times of the year left my husband feeling especially neglected. His unattainable needs were not as easily met during the hustle and bustle. I always knew that life would improve after the holidays, and this was a fairly predictable cycle. As a narcissistic abuse victim I found myself always waiting for the other shoe to drop, so to speak. And when it did, I patiently waited for the bread crumbs. As long as there were enough good days to cancel out the bad ones, then this relationship worked.

In my mind, one good day made up for one bad day. Never mind that the bad day might have resulted in emotional damage to me. If a good day followed, then I learned to forget the bad one. I was lowering my expectations with each passing year and I began to tolerate more frequent abusive behavior amid the tiny crumbs of bread.

Along with bread crumbing, narcissists also use gaslighting as a means of control. While the two terms are similar, gaslighting can be seen as much more sinister in nature. While it is a means to gain control, the main purpose of gaslighting is to make the victim feel crazy, like they are losing their mind. The narcissist will distort the truth, making the victim actually question their sanity. The phrase "gaslighting" comes from a 1938 stage play called Gas Light. In this play, a husband attempts to drive his young wife insane by dimming the gas powered lights in their home and then denying that the lights had changed when the wife pointed it out. Naturally, the young wife fears she might be going crazy. This type of emotional abuse gives the narcissist power over their victim. Narcissists will often say phrases like, "You're remembering that wrong," or "You're blowing it out of proportion, you're just too sensitive." The victim is left wondering if in fact their memory is deceiving them. Maybe it really wasn't that bad? Maybe I am over reacting? This was exactly what I did in the early days of my marriage. I convinced myself that I was over reacting. I was just too sensitive. I shouldn't let my husband's disrespect affect me so much. At least this is what I was conditioned to believe.

Victims of gaslighting will often be left feeling confused and may struggle to make simple decisions. This was me. I struggled with decisions because I feared making the wrong one. A simple decision could be a source of great anxiety for me. Gaslighting causes the victim to second guess themselves at every single turn. As a victim, I became very unsure of myself over the years. I learned to not trust my instincts for fear they could be deceiving me. Most narcissists are experts at this gaslighting technique and find it useful in protecting their ego, erasing "bad events" from their victim's supposed flawed memory, and in controlling the narrative. Narcissists, especially the covert kind, cannot afford to be unmasked. Their ego is far too important to them. Over time and after years of gaslighting I often found myself thinking I must be the crazy one. My husband consistently touted the narrative that he was the most amazing husband, he never did anything wrong and I should feel so lucky to be married to him. "It's hard to find a husband as good as me," he would often say. And he expected me to adamantly agree. I didn't feel any of these things, but his control over me and the narrative made me confused and afraid to speak out against him in any way. Surely my perception is warped. There was no other explanation.

He must be right and I must be wrong. This way of thinking allowed me to allow him to become relentless in his abuse.

6

Cruising the Rough Seas

About five years into our marriage my husband and I decided to go on our first cruise together to the Yucatan aboard the Norwegian Sea. I had never cruised before and it had been several years since he had been on a cruise vacation. We were excited for our seven day adventure. He told me about all the things we would do on the ship: the meals, the excursions, the shows. He made it sound so exciting. It was going to be a fantastic new experience. And it was fantastic... until about 3:00 AM the first night on the ship when I woke up violently ill. Sea sickness had set in and had awoken me from a deep sleep. I hadn't adequately planned for this, and while I had experienced motion sickness as a child, this was so much worse. I spent that night and the next day unable to hold down any food or drinks, and surprisingly my husband wasn't the least bit concerned. In fact, not only was he unconcerned, he was furious with me. I could tell by his quiet demeanor and that all too familiar empty, glassy look in his eyes, that I had just ruined the trip. We were supposed to be having fun. The around the clock kind of fun he expected. He had taken a week off of work for this trip, so I owed him the experience he desired. How could I be so selfishly sick, unable to eat and barely stand upright? I was ruining the experience for him. I told him I was sure I would be okay by the next day. Surely seasickness can't last more than a day? However, this wasn't good enough for him. His fun couldn't be interrupted.

He insisted on continuing with the onboard activities that day, regardless of my being sick, and I followed along trying to act okay so he wouldn't be angry. I sat with him while he enjoyed breakfast at one of the onboard cafes while the aroma of the food was making me nauseous. I was determined to have breakfast with him to keep him happy. I was supposed to be enjoying this cruise alongside him after all, and if I left him to dine alone he would be even angrier. After his meal we were off to participate in a dance class. I was beyond miserable, but I went to this event anyway. Dancing on an undulating ship; the perfect thing for seasickness. I lasted about half way through the class until I was a queasy mess. I finally told my husband to continue on with the class. I had to retreat to our cabin to lie down. I would go back to the room by myself. I just needed some time to rest. My husband, making his usual grandiose public display of caring, insisted on returning to the room with me; but all the while, out of the view of his audience, he was telling me how embarrassed he was. How embarrassing that his wife was sea sick. He further admonished me for his embarrassment over my leaving the dance class early. He kept continually chiding me that I was so weak. "Sea sickness is all in your head," he told me. He had spent much of his younger years deep sea fishing with his dad, and he had never been seasick. Therefore, according to his expertise, sea sickness must not be real. If it doesn't affect him then it shouldn't affect anyone. "You're just faking it, and you aren't really that sick," he stated. "You just don't want to have fun with me," he continued to rebuke in his petulant tone. I could only wish that I was faking it.

By mid afternoon my husband had become so frustrated with my lack of participation in this cruise that he decided we would get off the ship at the first port the next day, which would be Cozumel, Mexico, and we would return home. There was no need to continue with this trip. It was ruined by me. I was sick, so we should just go home and forget the whole thing. With my husband it was always all or nothing, black and white. He only dealt in absolutes. If things weren't going his way, we should just throw in the towel. As if I didn't feel bad enough, now I was distraught. I had ruined our cruise. But as sick as I was, there was nothing I could do.

Later that day my husband, in a shockingly rare moment of caring, finally took me to the onboard clinic; although I don't doubt it was more for his chance to call my bluff and prove I was over-reacting than my personal well-being. Interestingly enough, there were several people in the waiting room who were also seasick. I guess they were all faking it too, or at least that's what my husband must have thought. When it was my turn to be seen I was told by the nurse that I should feel better by the next day. No need to worry, she had said. She told me I would adjust to the movement of the ship and that I would be fine. She told me to just take it easy, and I was relieved. This malady wouldn't last the entire trip. There was hope for this cruise after all. My husband seemed a little more content hearing that, as it came from a medical staffer that he could not refute. Maybe, just maybe, there was a chance that he could salvage his fun and not take it out on me.

By that evening I was feeling marginally better after discovering a small miracle in one of the gift shops: small, elastic motion sickness bands. Once I put these bands on my wrists and placed them directly over my pressure points I had almost instant relief. I couldn't believe something so simple could make such a difference. I was pleasantly surprised, and I was actually able to go to dinner in the dining room. I chose a light meal and had some ginger ale to drink. By the next day, wearing a motion sickness band on each wrist, I was nearly back to normal. I was weak, but feeling well enough to actually begin enjoying the cruise. My husband was finally happy. He made no mention of returning home early. We were back on track, and I was relieved. We were on vacation and things were back to "normal," smooth sailing into the sunset. A crisis had been averted, and all was well in my husband's world once again.

Narcissists are known to lack empathy. However, they can put on an "empathic show" when it benefits them or when they need to look like the hero or the victim. Covert narcissists can be very deceiving and manipulative in the empathy department. While it's said that narcissists lack empathy, it is more accurate to say that they choose to not be empathetic. Like a faucet, most narcissists can turn their empathy on and off. Most are unwilling to see things from others' perspectives so they are only concerned with how a certain circumstance affects them. They are the most important person in the room. My husband chose not to empathize with my seasickness because to do so would impact him negatively. Caring for the welfare of another individual, even a so called "loved one," would keep him from a day of fun in the sun. So he chose to be angry instead. He wasn't concerned about my health in the least. He was only concerned about how my "health issue" affected him. In my marriage it was the same song and dance every time I found myself sick or injured. If it adversely impacted him it was cause for condemnation, not care. I was of no use to him if I was in bed sick. I wasn't seen as a person. I was an object. And I needed to be useful. If I couldn't be useful to him, my husband chose apathy. Having the flu would yield nothing but anger from my narcissistic husband. "Are you still sick?" he would say. "Are you sure you're not just faking it?" No compassion, no empathy, just apathy and sheer disgust.

In the later years of my marriage I found it easier to not discuss with my husband anything that would call for an empathetic response. If I had a problem I was dealing with I most often did not inform my husband. I internalized it. Instead of displaying empathy and compassion, he was very adept at making me feel even worse or telling me that his problems were much more important. He was the ultimate "one-upper." He would divert the conversation to himself every time, talking of stress at his job and how difficult his life was with so much responsibility. The responsibility of being so important, or at least feeling like he was, was indeed a tall order. I learned to keep most of my feelings to myself. I buried deep inside myself my feelings of anxiety, fear, my feelings of hopelessness and my panic attacks. It was just easier to never discuss these topics. These feelings made me look weak and worthless in his eyes, which I hated because for years I placed so much value on what he thought of me. He would often say things like, "You're always sick," and indeed I was sick a lot. Most of the sickness resulted from the stress that he was creating in my life and of having to suppress my internal feelings and fears.

These suppressed feelings found other ways to manifest. I was plagued with stomach problems and feeling nauseas far too often. Fatigue kept me worn down as well, but I tried not to make an issue of these ailments. I couldn't let him see me as weak. As a result, I found myself withdrawing more and more every day, almost living a secret life. I was miserable, not feeling well and experiencing panic much of the time. I managed to appear happy and well adjusted to the outside world for his benefit, but actually I was fighting my hardest battles and no one knew. I was wasting away so that he could have his perfect world. His happiness was sucking the life from me like a parasite.

7

A Negative Connection

So what exactly do narcissists look for in a partner? The answer is fairly simple. They look for those who are extremely empathetic, caring, willing to serve and compassionate. Narcissists choose people who are very forgiving, very lenient and very understanding; "people pleasers," you might say. Partners who are loyal to a fault. While these can be good traits, the narcissist capitalizes on the fact that these traits can also make a person more easily manipulated. By using their own traits against them, the narcissist makes the victim build their own cage and not even realize it.

Narcissists don't like boundaries if they are someone else's. In fact they hate boundaries because boundaries violate the idea that the narcissist is in control of everything and everyone. Empathetic people don't always have solid boundaries. Their boundaries can be so permeable that they can easily be compromised and broken down. Narcissists will also seek partners who are prone to guilt, or those who are easily shamed. This is a valuable trait and the narcissist will exploit it. All in all, the perfect partner for a narcissist is someone who will be willing to overlook the abuse. The perfect enabler. An unknowingly willing victim. Many of these traits, both good and bad, described me.

Growing up in the Bible Belt of midwest America I lived a rather sheltered life in a beautiful home in the country. I attended a small, rural school and had good friends and lots of family around me. I didn't know anyone with a "personality disorder." I wasn't very cultured and it never ever dawned on me that someone could manipulate another person to the point of abuse. I was a typical naive teenage girl and I couldn't fathom that such people existed. The sad truth is, no one is raised to be cautious of the narcissist around the corner. No one is taught to beware of the red flags of narcissistic abuse. I had never heard of such a thing. I had never dealt with people who were overly conniving, overly controlling, or those possessing sinister agendas. I idyllically believed people to be inherently good.

I was naive about many things and my lack of worldly knowledge was appealing to my narcissistic husband. He saw this as easy access for control. I was kind; too kind in fact. He saw early on that I would forgive his missteps and that I would be loyal even in the face of abuse. I was too accommodating, making sure to the best of my abilities that he was always happy. Perhaps the best quality, and most advantageous to him, that he saw in me was that I was always willing to take the blame. He loved this. He could convince me I had done something wrong even when it was he who had made a mistake. In my need to please him, I fell for it every time. After all, narcissists don't make mistakes. My husband zeroed in on these qualities when we were dating. I was just what he needed, as I could provide his supply. I was his never ending supply of admiration, attention, praise, and the like. I was deemed a valuable asset. I had been targeted and vetted. My "good" qualities were used against me and by the early years of my marriage I had no boundaries left. Not weakened boundaries, but no boundaries. This is quite simply a narcissist's dream scenario.

As much as I wanted to experience a deep and emotional connection with my husband, it seemed impossible to find any kind of emotional attachment with him. That side of him didn't seem to exist. At least I couldn't find it. I surmised that after a little more time together I might find that connection. Maybe these things take time, so I was patient. However, all I could find was what seemed to be a superficial side, surface-level and a bit shallow. He wasn't seeking a bond with me, and perhaps he wasn't capable of any kind of connection. Ours was not an equal partnership, after all. Instead, it was an unbalanced scale where I ended up feeling like a servant and he was the king. It was a perfectly convenient arrangement for him. I was just another piece of property that served to worship him. As long as I complied and didn't deface the fraudulent mask my husband was showing to the outside world, in his mind we could live happily ever after. We were the perfect couple in his twisted up world.

Master and servant. He provided me with financial security, all the material things that I could want, and a very comfortable life. I owed him. And he owned me.

8

Urgent Care

About 12 years into my marriage I began having physical symptoms as a result of the continual stress I was under from trying to survive the situation in which I was living. One of these symptoms was heart palpitations. My heart was skipping beats much too frequently. I had begun having these fluttering skips regularly one January, just after the holidays. Holidays are always stressful in their own way, but when you add in a narcissistic spouse the stress level magnifies ten-fold. While my irregular, fluttering heartbeats would come and go at times, this particular time they didn't appear to be going anywhere. The constant stress of keeping my husband as the most important person in the world, had my heart skipping relentlessly. After several days of near constant palpitations I decided I should visit my nearest urgent care just to get checked out. I had my 18 month old in his stroller, and I wasn't sure exactly how this was going to work, but I knew it was time to seek medical attention.

Once I got settled into a hospital bed I called my husband. His wife was in urgent care. Any normal person would be a nervous wreck when they found out that kind of news. To my surprise though, my husband had already left work for the afternoon. He had been dealing with some sinus congestion for the past week and he had secured a doctor's appointment that very same afternoon. "I'm at urgent care. I'm worried there's something wrong with my heart." I pleaded with him, "I have the baby here with me. Can you come?" No, he couldn't. His head congestion was making him miserable and he wasn't about to give up his doctor's appointment. "I'm sick too. I'm at the doctor's office," he said. Granted, sinus congestion is not pleasant, but neither is thinking you might be having a heart attack. It's not even in the same category. My fear and my life were not important enough for him to make even a small effort to see if I was okay; not to mention I had my infant son with me. My husband was not only abandoning me in this moment, he was abandoning his son too. His head congestion was more important than the welfare of his wife and child. Fortunately, my baby was content in his stroller munching on Cheerios while I was hooked up to an assortment of beeping monitors. I decided there was nothing I could do except relax, or at least try to under the circumstances. But thinking about him just leaving us there and his total lack of concern made that a true challenge. Did I really mean so little to him? Was my life of so little value to the man I thought loved me?

After an hour or so of monitoring I received some good news. My EKG had came back okay. My heart rate was all over the place, but I was definitely not having a heart attack. The peace of mind this gave me made me feel somewhat better. The doctor wanted to keep me for another hour, just to watch my heart rhythm as an extra precaution. But that created another problem. It was coming up on 3:00 PM, and that meant school was getting ready to release. My first grader was counting on my car to be in the car line at pickup time. I made another call to my husband. "Can you do car line? It's almost 3:00, and the doctor wants to monitor me for a little bit longer." No, he couldn't. He was heading to the pharmacy to pick up some over the counter medications for his congestion. He needed to go home and rest. After all, he had had a hard day at work and he was feeling lousy. He just didn't have the energy to pick our daughter up from school. Now we were all three being abandoned.

I couldn't think of a single other person to call and 3:00 was fast approaching. I made a quick decision, as it was my only option at that time. I checked myself out of urgent care against the doctor's orders. The nurse was baffled. "Can't you find someone to pick up your daughter?" she said. I told her no, embarrassed to have anyone see me bowing down to the whims of a tyrant. All I could do was mutter, "I have to leave now." The nurse reluctantly proceeded to unhook my monitors and gave me a form to sign. I had to verify that I understood I was checking out of the clinic against doctor's orders. Yes, I understood, but I had no choice. I also understood that I wasn't having a heart attack and that my first grader needed a ride home. I gathered my things and what dignity I had left, loaded up my son in the car and headed to the school, arriving just in the nick of time. I put on a brave face for my daughter so she would not be worried.

My kids and I arrived home where we found my husband already tucked away in bed with no obvious concerns regarding my health, my visit to the urgent care, or if our daughter had been safely picked up from school. I was furious and I could feel my heart fluttering again. What I felt was a mix of anger, embarrassment and worthlessness. The latter I felt most of all. Our evening routine played out as usual. I fed the kids dinner, helped with homework and got everyone to bed. The reassurance I had gotten from the doctor that afternoon provided a little consolation to ease my mind. My physical heart was going to be okay, and eventually the palpitations would subside. But my proverbial heart was in a million pieces.

9

Social Security

Verbal abuse wasn't uncommon in our house. My husband had very little, if any, tolerance for honest mistakes and a condescending speech almost always followed. He loved to talk at length about how he was the expert in whatever topic was on the table. He knew more than anyone about anything and he felt that his lectures were very valuable. He thought I could stand to learn a lot from his vast knowledge of all things, and mistakes made by me or others were deeply frowned upon. My husband, however, was allowed to make as many mistakes as he needed to, honest or not. His mistakes were not a problem, just a minor inconvenience. However, anyone else's mistakes, especially mine, were earth shattering,.

A few years into our marriage we made a move to a new state for my husband's job. I had to get a new drivers license and my husband was helping me retrieve all my documents from our safe the evening before. I didn't want to arrive at the DMV and not have an item that I needed, so to be on the safe side I planned to take everything- Birth Certificate, Social Security card, passport, everything I could possibly need to obtain my new driver's license. My trip to the DMV was a success the following day and I returned home with my documents in hand. At least I was pretty sure I had.

The documents were in a plastic sleeve, and I had placed them on the kitchen counter, ready to be returned to the safe. Later that evening, after my husband had deposited these important items back in their secure spot, he questioned where my Social Security card was. "It was in the plastic sleeve alongside my other documents," I said. He replied that it was not. Only my birth certificate and passport had been returned to him. He decided that I must have left my Social Security card at the DMV. "You dropped it," he admonished. "You're always so careless and irresponsible with these things." After carefully searching my car and my purse, it was clear that the card had not made it back home with me. My husband decided that I had made a terrible, irredeemable mistake and proceeded to inform me of all the problems this act of negligence would cause. Identity theft was at the top of his list. He explained, as to a child, the issues that I would be faced with. Always the alarmist, he told me my life could be ruined because of this irresponsible and foolish act I had just committed. He told me I would need to prepare to fight an identity theft case for several years. These things were not easily resolved. Someone out there had my social security number and they were going to do countless illegal things in my name. This was all my fault for being so stupidly irresponsible.

I didn't know what to do. I had been so careful with my documents. I was crushed and humiliated. I guess I had really dropped this card at the DMV and there was no telling who had it now. I was in tears, and he had no sympathy for me, only sheer disgust. How careless and stupid could I be? He informed me I would need to go back to the DMV the next day and launch a search for this coveted card. I agreed. I had really messed up. I was literally sick, thinking about all the problems I had just caused for myself and, of course, for my husband. How could I have been so irresponsible? I was pretty sure, based on my husband's lengthy sermon, that this must be the worst mistake I had ever made.

I asked my husband just before heading to bed that night if we could check the safe one more time. Maybe, just maybe, the card was in that plastic sleeve. I was sure I had been very careful. Maybe he had just missed it? Maybe he had made a mistake and just overlooked it? He said it absolutely was not in the safe. He had already checked and he was thorough. In fact, he was the most thorough person in our household. Nothing would ever get by him. Begrudgingly, after much pleading on my part, he decided to open the safe. With a few clicks the door opened, and my husband pulled out the plastic sleeve he had placed inside just a few hours earlier. He emptied the contents onto his desk, and there was the little green Social Security card, tucked inside my passport. Still in tears, I was now beyond relieved. My life wouldn't be ruined by an identity thief after all. I hadn't lost the card. I hadn't been irresponsible. I could breathe a little easier.

I figured my husband would apologize for his sermon, his chiding, his humiliating me. I had been in a panic, in tears, and extremely distressed after his lengthy decimation of my character. This was his mistake, after all. He had failed to see the card and had blamed me for losing it. However, I was shocked when I saw his response. He didn't apologize. He didn't accept responsibility. He didn't admit he may have overreacted. He never recanted his accusatory statement of me being stupidly irresponsible. It was as if none of those things happened. Instead, to my surprise, he laughed. He laughed at himself. How silly of him to have missed my card among my other documents! It was no big deal, not to him. It was funny! It was a simple mistake on his part. He, and only he, was allowed to make mistakes with no apologies, reprimands or consequences. Another crisis had been averted and everything was fine. He closed the safe and thought nothing more about the situation. Just an "honest" mistake. His mistake, the only kind that was allowed and accepted in his universe in which he was the center.

10

The Complexity of Cashew Chicken

Narcissists tend to be extremely jealous, as well as believing others are extremely jealous of them. They are the center of their own universe, and they expect everyone and everything to revolve around them. Narcissists want to dominate your time and your energy. No person or thing deserves more admiration and attention than they do. They are the god of their own religion and all things should worship them. It's not unusual for narcissists to even become jealous of their own children.

One day, our family had decided to try a new Chinese restaurant. It was a beautiful day, everyone was happy, and it should have been a pleasant experience. However, we had a narcissist in our party. This particular restaurant had counter service. The menus were posted at the beginning of the line. As we entered, we were all reading our options and deciding what we wanted so that we would be ready to order when it was our turn at the counter. I was helping our children, ages 6 and 10, decide what to get. There were many delicious options and combinations and the kids and I were deciding if they wanted to split an order or order two separate meals. Once that was all decided, my husband said to me, "Well, aren't you going to help me now?" I thought, "Help you do what? Help you read the menu?" This was a full grown man, with a college degree, and he wanted me to step him through each menu item and decipher the complexity of cashew chicken. He immediately saw the look of confusion on my face and followed up by stating, "Well you helped the kids." I immediately shot back with a response. "Yeah, they're kids," I said. That was a critical error on my part.

Now his feelings were hurt. I wouldn't help him order. I was actually asking him to order for himself, and he couldn't believe it. I had defied him and I had done it in public. With that, he puffed up, said he didn't understand the menu, and he made a spectacle of stepping out of line to go and sit down. A masters degree in engineering, and he couldn't figure out how to order Chinese food. He just wasn't going to eat; just another childish tantrum because I wouldn't take the time to help him, and he was appalled. I quickly saw where this was going. Our lunch was about to be ruined, and he wouldn't hesitate to make a bigger scene in public if it meant getting his point across. He always got his point across, no matter who he embarrassed or intimidated. He wouldn't even hesitate to unknowingly make a fool of himself. I had to act quickly to avoid the inevitable. So, like so many times before, I caved. I caught him just as he was exiting the line and beginning his grand performance as a martyr to the injustice of being married to such an insensitive wife. As if talking to a child, I said, "Here, let me help you decide what to order." And I did. I explained the various combinations on the menu and discussed the variety of flavors from which he could choose. I showed him the same level of attention that I had shown to my young children. Oddly enough, this satisfied him. When we had finally made his meal selection, I stepped up to the counter and ordered lunch for our family.

My husband was pleased with himself for getting what he wanted. The angered god had been placated. He was finally happy. But I wasn't. I had just jumped through yet another hoop to make sure he stayed happy and content. I decided it was better than the alternative. Any submission I gave was better than the alternative. I was looking at a possible scene in the restaurant, pouting for hours, days of the silent treatment... It wasn't worth it. It wasn't worth the embarrassment to myself and my children. In my world it was always the best decision to hold it together and bow down. For the sake of my children, it was my job to keep the family running smoothly and constantly remind myself, "Whatever you do, don't trigger him..."

II

Fear Factors

Fear is a favorite tactic often used by narcissists. That four letter word holds so much crippling power. It is their ace in the hole, their trump card, and my husband knew how to use it to his advantage in any given situation. In retrospect I'm not sure he even knew how much power his fear inducing behavior gave him over me, but if he did I'm sure he would be quite proud of himself. Fear of physical injury on myself, fear that he would injure himself, fear that he would abandon us; these are the types of fear that he instilled in our family. He was never physical to me, at least not directly, but there was always a lingering fear that he, in fact, could be.

In the car, if he became upset over something that I or the kids did or said, his response was to start driving recklessly. He would drive at excessive speeds, quickly changing lanes in an attempt to induce terror. He was actually a good driver, and he knew he wasn't going to crash the car, but he enjoyed the life-threatening fear that he could manufacture by being insanely reckless. The power he held over our very lives gave him a high like it was the most powerful narcotic in the world. He enjoyed seeing me on edge, and if he could induce an anxiety attack in me, it was just another win for him. It put a feather in his proverbial cap. He wanted everyone in the car to know that he had the power to end us in a heartbeat.

One Saturday when our kids were about 8 and 12 our family was on a short day trip. The kids were in the backseat and the car stereo was playing. Our daughter had been a music lover from a very young age and listening to music in the car was one of her favorite activities. So while we were cruising on down the road she asked her dad to turn up the radio. There was a song on that she liked, probably a One Direction song, and she wanted to hear it louder in the backseat. He ignored her request. He would say in his defense that he was concentrating on the road. Maybe so, but I always played the radio loud in the car when I was the driver and the kids loved it. My daughter mistakingly assumed that her dad would do the same. She asked him to increase the volume a few more times because that is what pre-teen children do. Then finally he snapped.

I'll never know why this caused such enraged frustration in him, but he slammed on the brakes and the car screeched to a halt, sending all four of us in motion. Thank goodness for seat-belts, or one or more of us would have been seriously injured.

There we were, on a two lane road, stopped in the middle of the lane. My husband, red-faced, yelled a few expletive words and then turned the stereo up to an ear drum bursting volume. At this point no one wanted to hear music, even if it was One Direction. My husband had turned this car trip into a dangerously reckless scene and scared us all. The rest of our ride was in silence, as we were all too terrified to make a sound. He was the driver, he had the wheel, and we just wanted to arrive at our destination in one piece. He had gone from zero to furious in no time, and he was in a position to make sure we knew he was in power. Deadly sure.

Creating a panic situation was evidence to my husband that he was personally in control of my emotions, and he aspired to control everything. When he was in control of the car I was powerless. He was behind the wheel and he was making the decisions. It gave him a huge rush to feel so empowered. It was just another way to get his point across; one of the many ways to let me know he was unhappy with me or the kids. It was a sadistic way for him to control the kids' behavior and make them stop arguing or bickering in the backseat. His solution was simply to scare everyone and let us all know that our lives were in his hands. He had the power to wreck the car and injure us all if he was so inclined, and we all knew that. A car is a powerful and deadly weapon when it's in the wrong hands, and an angry narcissist's hands should never be on a steering wheel. Intimidation with a motor vehicle, as I later would learn, isn't uncommon for narcissists and is actually considered physical abuse. After all, the person controlling the wheel is certainly capable of bodily injury or causing death.

A non-physical indirect fear tactic that is also common with narcissists is to throw or destroy things, and my husband would do both. Hurling an object through the air, creating a loud clattering noise, was intimidating. It let everyone in the house know that he was unhappy, like an overgrown toddler who was denied what he wanted. Only it isn't just annoyingly typical and easy to accept like with a toddler's tantrum. It is recklessly terrifying when a full grown adult begins destroying everything around them in a fury induced rage tornado. It was important for my husband that I knew in no uncertain terms when he was unhappy. He would throw anything that might be in his hand. He would never throw an object directly at someone. That circumstance would be harder to hide, especially if his actions caused someone injury. However, he would be sure to throw the object hard enough to cause damage, make a loud noise and scare everyone in the house. He had to induce the right amount of shock and awe to produce fear.

One day after getting upset with our young children who were bickering, my husband threw an aerosol can of glass cleaner that he just happened to have in his hand at the very moment the kids began to argue. He hurled it right at our wooden staircase, knocking a chuck of wood out of one of the steps. The room immediately became silent as the cloud of fear gripped us all. This permanently damaged the step, though later he would disclaim that his immature action created this damage. He knew he had done it, though, and he was most likely secretly proud of his work. Interestingly enough, he never repaired that step. I often wondered if he left it there as a reminder of his power; a monument not to his immaturity, but to his rule as king of the house and his ultimate authority. Narcissists, like my husband, want to be the center of attention and when they create a loud ruckus by throwing or destroying an object, they most definitely gain the attention of everyone. Look at me! I'm not getting my way!

It is said that narcissists have the emotional maturity of a toddler. On many days I felt certain that my husband had never advanced past the age of three. Behind closed doors his emotions could indeed run wild and his ability to regulate his emotions was stunted. A grown man throwing a toddler-style temper tantrum is a sight to behold. Although it can be hilarious to watch at first, it can be fear inducing in its madness and unpredictability. Unfortunately this kind of behavior is common in narcissism. Throwing an unreasonable fit until everyone gives in is a means to an end for them- especially if their fit can involve some intimidation.

Fear of abandonment is yet another favorite card a narcissist will play, and it is an incredibly powerful one. They threaten to leave if they don't get what they want, almost like a young child threatening to run away from home. With a child, you know this can be an empty threat that is done to test your resolve as a parent. However, when it is an adult using it against a spouse or significant other, it attacks your value as a partner and uses your love for the person making the threat against you to make you succumb. My husband did this on more than one occasion, and it always caused a major disruption in our family. Of course, this was his goal. Disrupt our lives until he gets what he wants.

One year when the kids were young, my husband left our family two days before Christmas. He literally walked out on us. He said he wasn't coming back for the holiday. We would have to manage without him. My first thought was that we might actually have a peaceful Christmas. An actual "silent night." But then reality began to set in and I thought about my family. I had to be reasonable and once again I thought about damage control. We had to be together for Christmas, playing the part of the happy family. Even if we weren't the all American family that we represented on our annual Christmas card, we could at least act like we were. What would people say? One would imagine that my husband's sudden and emotional departure must have resulted from a huge domestic dispute. But remember, we are dealing with a narcissist, and their reaction rarely matches the "crime." The event that precipitated such a brash backlash was this: our two young children had been quarreling, which is something children everywhere have been doing for centuries. They were arguing over our plans for the day. One of them wanted to attend a Christmas event that our church was hosting and the other one wanted to stay home. They were frustrated with one another because one kid would ultimately have to concede to the other. Peace in the Middle East would have been an easier obtainable goal. My husband didn't deserve this, in his opinion. He deserved a peaceful home. No chaos, no children fighting. He deserved his perfect Norman Rockwell

Christmas. Our home should look like a Hollywood movie. In fact, his entire life should look like a Hollywood movie. He was better than this. He shouldn't have to deal with children's disagreements, unplanned chaos or unforeseen circumstances. It cramped his style. The universe owed him a perfect Christmas because he thought it should, and nothing was going to get in the way of that. He therefore decided he would teach us all a lesson and walk out, abandoning us just before Christmas. And that's exactly what he did. He packed a bag, loudly exclaimed that he was leaving, got into his car and drove to a nearby hotel where he spent the night.

I will admit, after the shock of his huge scene, there was a sense of relief when he drove away. For a moment I could relax. I could breathe. I could sort out the kids' disagreement myself, which actually turned out to not be a big deal. But then it was time to do the damage control, and once again I had to cave to my husband's behavior. I couldn't let him leave our family at Christmas. What would I tell the kids? What was even going through their minds? I let it go for the night and decided to have an enjoyable evening with my son and daughter. There was no way I was going to let them think that their father abandoning them on Christmas was their fault. Our house was quiet and peaceful. We ordered a Dominoes pizza and some chocolate lava cakes for dessert and piled onto the living room couch to watch a movie.

When the next morning came I had to do something. As much as it pained me, I called my husband and apologized. I took the blame, as usual. I recited my usual placating spiel. It's my fault. I'm an inadequate parent. I shouldn't allow the kids to quarrel so much because I know it causes you stress, and so on and so on. I degraded myself thoroughly with the usual groveling and made him feel as though we couldn't celebrate Christmas without him. Once he was convinced that the kids and I were desperate and broken enough he decided he would return home. I had bowed down to him again. This is what I had to do, or so I thought, and I always did what I had to do to keep the peace. While he was seemingly angry and frustrated with me for the rest of the day, I think he actually enjoyed every second of it. He was exerting his power through fear and intimidation and he was winning. He got what he wanted for Christmas.

My husband would often threaten to hurt himself. This again is a common and disturbing antic of the narcissist. Play the victim role in any situation. If you can make everyone feel sorry for you then you'll get your way. The suicide card was always in his deck, and he would play it if he felt like he was beginning to lose control. If I didn't start paying more attention to him, if I didn't make him an even greater priority, if I didn't please him as a wife, then he wasn't sure if he wanted to continue living. His happiness, his life, his livelihood was in my hands, and I honestly didn't want this kind of responsibility. It was a lie. He would in no way give anyone control over any aspect of his life, but I was made to think I was in charge of his very existence if I did not comply. I took him seriously. What else could I do? It was a false responsibility that was put onto me.

A threat of suicide is a serious threat, not to be undermined or made in jest. But it was also the ultimate manipulation tactic for my husband. The choice was as simple as it was heavy: be a better wife, or I'll kill myself. All I could think was how I didn't want to be responsible for his demise. This threat also made me question my worth as a person. Was I such a horrible human being that someone could choose to end their life over my actions? How could I ever live with myself? What would I tell his family, my family, our kids? This was a devious tactic that was designed to attack my naivety and my self worth. It would be my fault if he went through with it, and I couldn't let that happen. I wouldn't let it happen. So when all else failed in my husband's world, he knew he could play the suicide card and it would work every single time. Why did it work? Because I allowed it to work every single time. He got his way every time he played this coveted trump card. It was the ultimate fear tactic, and he knew it. He most definitely wasn't afraid to use it. He took pleasure in instilling fear in me. Threatening suicide was a tactic that caused terror, and he was well aware of this. If he went through with it, it would turn my entire world upside down, leave my children and myself alone, destroy my self worth as a wife and mother and it would all be my fault. Calling his bluff was just too much to risk. His tactic worked every time because I feared having my world destroyed by "my own actions." That fear, my fear, was his most effective tool.

10 Questions

Ten questions to ask yourself if you think you might be in an emotionally abusive relationship:

1. Does your partner get upset when you do not comply with their ideals or plans?
2. Do you endure the silent treatment?
3. Are you responsible for their feelings and their self-esteem?
4. Are you accused of rejecting them when you take time to do something for yourself?
5. Does your partner often put you down or degrade you so that you no longer feel good about yourself?
6. Do you feel as if you have no rights in the relationship?
7. Do you tell your partner what they want to hear to avoid repercussions?
8. Do you fear saying or doing the wrong thing in front of your partner?
9. Do you walk on eggshells?
10. Do you feel unsafe and insecure around your partner?

These are all signs of a very unhealthy and emotionally abusive relationship. Answering yes to even one of these questions warrants a closer look into the partnership. Early in my marriage I could have answered an emphatic yes to each of these 10 questions, but in those earlier years I didn't realize these questions represented an abusive dynamic. I didn't realize I was taking on way too much responsibility in my marriage. I wasn't seeking answers to these types of questions. I didn't know enough about emotional abuse to even ask these questions to myself. Instead I was accepting my situation as normal. I had become complacent. The resources were there for me, but I didn't know I needed help, and I wouldn't realize my extreme need for several more years. I would have to witness a lot more volatility in my marriage before I would ultimately begin pursuing answers.

I 2

Penguins

When our children were about 7 and 11 my husband and I decided to take a weekend family trip. There was a wonderful aquarium and resort about two hours from our home, and we had heard they offered a penguin encounter that sounded exciting and unique. The kids were thrilled. We were going to interact with macaroni penguins up close and personal! We made the drive to this nearby town and checked into our beautiful hotel room. We were ready for a weekend of fun. Penguins, the aquarium, an I-Max movie and lots of good food. Our first stop was lunch at the resort. We took the kids to a casual cafe and ordered the usual staples- chicken fingers and french fries, burgers and the like. My 7 year old son ordered the kids chicken finger meal. My husband ordered the adult chicken finger meal. Same meal, just different quantities of food. When the young server delivered our lunch to the table he mistakingly mixed up the chicken finger plates. My son was given the adult portion and my husband was given, to his disgust, the kids portion.

I should divert here to mention that my seven year old son had recently been diagnosed with a form of high functioning autism. He was an empathic and sensitive child, all in good ways, but he couldn't handle changes in routines. The slightest hiccup could precipitate a total meltdown, and these meltdowns might last for hours. My son had trouble regulating his emotions when he encountered a stressful situation, but I was already accustomed to this before my son came along. I had had several years of meltdown training as a result of living with a narcissist. I was up to the task. While I walked on eggshells around my husband, I was also careful not to knowingly create a meltdown opportunity for my son. It was an acrobatic feat most days. I felt like I was walking a tightrope with no netting underneath me. It was my daily routine, however, and most days I was proficient. But not every day.

So, back to our lunch table.... I could see quickly that my husband was on edge. I knew if I switched the plates, my son's day could be completely disrupted, which in turn would disrupt everyone's day. It was a conundrum. I was trying to keep the family happy. We were on vacation. We were going to see penguins, after all. I explained to my husband that the two plates were identical. Same food, different quantities. Anyone with an ounce of sense could see this. I explained to my husband that my son would not finish all of his chicken fingers. There were too many, and my son ate like a bird. I said to my husband, "Just eat what's on your plate, and when he's done you can have the rest of his chicken. No big deal." Oh, but it was an enormous deal to my husband. It was the biggest deal in the world. He jumped up and abruptly left the table. I was shocked, but tried to act un-phased in front of the kids. My husband had actually just gotten up and walked out of the restaurant over chicken fingers. His son had more chicken fingers than he had, and I didn't correct the problem. In that moment I could not believe what my life had been reduced to. I had two children, but in that moment I actually had three children. Everyone else in the cafe was enjoying their food. I looked around at all of the "normal" families eating lunch together, smiling, laughing, and talking. But not mine. My husband, acting like a spoiled child, was fuming.

After he had stormed out, he exited the building and waited outside for us to finish our lunch, which we did. "Don't worry about dad," I said to the kids, "Just eat your lunch." I quickly finished my meal, not eating much because my husband's behavior had spoiled my appetite and potentially the whole weekend.

I left the table to go outside and speak with this man who was acting like a toddler. He'd had some time to cool off and regain his composure, or so I thought. I had thought wrong. "I'm going back home. I'm taking the car. I don't know how you and the kids will get home, but you can figure something out." Huh? My husband was going to leave his family stranded at a resort two hours from home with no vehicle, all because he had been served a children's portion at lunch? I did my best to convince him to stay. "Don't do this to the kids," I told him.

He was silent, and I wasn't sure what he would ultimately do. I was experiencing my all too normal sense of panic. I had no idea what the rest of this trip was going to look like and the uncertainty made me exceedingly anxious.

I went back into the cafe as the kids were finishing their meal. I proceeded to explain to them that dad might have to go back home, but I assured them that we would continue on with our plans to see the penguins. They were confused, to say the least. Why would dad want to change our plans? We had all been looking forward to this weekend and we were here to have fun. I tried to play it cool. No big deal, no stress. Our weekend was going to continue as planned. I had no idea how the kids and I would get home, but I would worry about that catastrophe later. After all, we had penguins to visit.

As we headed to the aquarium after lunch my husband begrudgingly followed along, clearly angry and pouting. He said very little, making sure I knew he was upset. The kids were relentless. "Dad, are you really leaving? I thought you wanted to go to the aquarium with us," and on and on. And then I added in my two cents, as well, making sure he knew I wanted him to continue the weekend with us. What I really wanted, however, was a guaranteed ride home. I couldn't imagine telling my children that we were stranded and it was all due to their father and the amount of chicken fingers he had been served at the cafe. Ultimately we all begged him enough, which is just what he wanted. He wanted to be begged, to feel important and to feel like we just couldn't manage without him. "Dad, you HAVE to come see the penguins," the kids continued. And so he did.

We learned about penguins, encountered one up close and even got to watch the penguin create art while he hopped across a series of canvases with paint on his little feet. At the end of the demonstration my husband bought two canvases for the kids, and they were thrilled. Happiness exuded, but all I could think of was my husband's behavior at lunch. However, I did a great job of faking joy once again, all for the sake of the kids.

My husband seemed happy that he had elected to stay with his family for the weekend, and he had actually enjoyed the activities. He was perhaps happiest with the fact that he had won, again. Everyone in the family, not just me, had caved this time, begging and pleading for his presence, making him feel like the most important member of the family.

13

An RV Trip

Our family had always marveled at the idea of an RV vacation. We had seen such trips played out in the movies and on TV. It seemed like a great memory making experience. So one spring break when the kids were about 8 and 12, we decided to rent an RV and drive to Las Vegas with a planned stop at the Grand Canyon on the way. We let our kids each pick a Vegas show to see and we purchased tickets for our family. My daughter chose Cirque du Soleil and my son chose David Copperfield. This was going to be our best vacation to date. It would be an all new experience for everyone. We went to pick up the RV the day before heading out, and my husband filled out all the necessary paperwork. He would be the driver of the vehicle, as the paperwork showed. That evening we spent several hours loading up and preparing the RV for our expedition. The next day we would head out bright and early. Our drive to Las Vegas would take 3 days with all of our planned stops along the way. It would be a lot of driving, but my husband assured us all that he was up to the task. This would be a great family trip.

Our drive was pleasant. The kids took turns sitting in the front passenger captain's seat while their dad drove. And when they weren't sitting in the front, they were in the back watching a movie or playing a board game with me at the table. My husband drove and I kept the kids entertained. It seemed like a good system, and everyone was happy, for the most part. We enjoyed a day at the Grand Canyon and spent some time touring Hoover Dam. So far, so good. And then we arrived in Las Vegas. We parked the RV and checked into our room at the beautiful Mandalay Bay Resort. To our surprise, we found that we had been upgraded to an even larger, nicer room in the hotel. The kids were excited about our upgrade and the plan was to unpack and get changed for dinner. The kids had heard us talk about the wonderful food and buffets in Las Vegas and everyone was hungry and ready to enjoy a huge dinner. Everyone except my husband.

Upon arriving in our hotel room my husband informed me that he wasn't having a good time. Up until this point I was pretty sure our trip had been a success, so I was taken aback at his proclamation. My husband stated that he was angry because he had to do all the driving on this trip. Apparently, he had failed to remember that he was the only authorized driver on the RV contract. That didn't matter. As he saw it, he drove and did all the work while the rest of us "played." Then he asked a question that perplexed me. "What are you going to do about it?" he asked. I was speechless. What did he expect me to do about it? Somehow, I guess, I was supposed to "fix" the fact that he wasn't having a good time. "I have no idea how to answer that question," I replied to my husband. With that response, he decided that this trip was not going to be fair. He had been slighted, once again, and he announced that he would be skipping the buffet dinner that we had planned. He would just stay in the room and sulk. And if that wasn't enough to shake up the mood of our trip, he then announced that he was also going to bow out of both Vegas shows, for which we had already purchased tickets. He didn't feel like going. This trip wasn't going to be fun. He was finished. It wasn't all about him, so he would just sit and pout while the kids and I continued on with the planned schedule.

I was absolutely baffled. I was so sure that we were all having a fantastic time, but apparently we weren't. After all, my husband's mood tended to dictate everyone's mood. If he was happy, everyone needed to be happy along with him. And if he was feeling hurt or upset, then he would make sure everyone else in the family also suffered. It was clear that the mood of our trip was about to get a lot worse. My husband was going to have a pity party for himself, the lone driver of the RV. I knew that the kids wouldn't easily understand what was going on, and I didn't feel like explaining to them that their dad would rather pout than enjoy Las Vegas with the family. I attempted to show my husband some sympathy, but I was at a loss. He wanted everyone to thank him for his hard work behind the wheel. He wanted to be told what a good driver he had been. He had sacrificed his happiness for the sake of his family. At least this was how he reasoned it.

"You're seriously not coming to dinner with us?" I asked my husband. I couldn't believe his outrageous behavior. I informed him that we had spent a good amount of money on show tickets and attractions and that the kids and I would continue on without him if need be. There was no way we would sit in the hotel room and watch him feel sorry for himself. We had driven too far for this level of nonsense. I told the kids it was time for dinner and my husband, with a loud sigh, announced that he was also coming. Of course he was coming. He wasn't about to miss out on the food or the fun. But he had seen an opportunity to acquire sympathy and he took it in grand fashion, as he always did.

My husband spent the rest of the trip having fun, but never failing to let me remember that he was the one "doing all the work" on the trip. We should all be thankful to him for being so selfless. In his mind he had taken us on vacation. Apparently it wasn't a vacation for him. He was such a good husband and father for playing the chauffeur role for his family, and he expected praise all around. Our family thoroughly enjoyed the shows and the sites of Vegas, and we made some fun memories along the way. However, my husband's underlying and unspoken attitude dampened the mood of the whole trip for me. I still managed to have fun and it did in fact go down as one of our more entertaining excursions- as entertaining as it could be with a narcissist complaining every mile of the way. It was crystal clear to me that our family would never again embark on another RV trip.

"*To ignore or use silence is a cruel tool. Hence this quote: Silence is all we dread; there's ransom in a voice; but silence is infinity.*"

- Emily Dickinson

14

A Loaded Gun

The silent treatment was a tactic often used by my husband when he was upset with me. He would use the tactics of silence and stonewalling to completely ignore me as if I did not even exist. Denying me the fundamental need to belong, to feel secure and safe, just to bend me to his will. The silent treatment is just what it sounds like- silence. It is a passive aggressive form of abuse that packs a punch but can be subtle at the same time. The abuser can use this form of manipulation in public or in private and it isn't always obvious to the casual observer. It is secret abuse, covert in delivery. Only you and your abuser know what is actually going on. It is a way to crush someone from the inside without laying a finger on them.

Because of the effectiveness of this tactic, and my need to be a good wife, I always found this form of abuse to cause me to examine my own behavior, rather than the abusive behavior of my husband. I would focus on what I had done to earn this treatment, how I had angered him and how I needed to change my actions to trigger him less. As a result, the blame shifted. Instead of blaming him for his manipulation, I blamed myself for triggering and failing him. And this is exactly the response he hoped for each time he used the silent treatment against me. This treatment would make me feel so unstable that I would do most anything to get things back on track again. His silent treatment was extremely silent. If I asked him a question he would literally pretend not to have heard me. My words were unheard and I was unseen. I was a ghost in my own life. No one wants to feel invisible; he knew this, and it gave him power.

My feelings of inadequacy would often result in my giving in and apologizing, even though there was nothing to apologize for. I simply couldn't stand the awkwardness and hopelessness of living in a house with someone who was pretending I didn't exist. It was not sustainable. How could a man who claimed he loved me keep me in a prison of invisible walls made of apathy? Apologizing seemed like the lesser of evils, the easiest and quickest way to avert the awkwardness, and give me back a shred of my self-value. I would ultimately end up saying things like, "I'm sorry I spent so much time reading that book yesterday. I should have spent that time with you." Caving in, once again, to restore the peace and gain back my self-worth. Admitting that I should never take time for myself was also acceptable to my abuser; admitting that I was treating him unfairly and that I could do better. I would apologize for nothing whatsoever if it meant being treated as if I was a human being in my own home and marriage.

One day about 18 years into my marriage I gathered the courage to put my foot down and not give in to my husband's silent treatment. It was the start of a rather interesting and frightening event. I had had it with the silent treatment. Hours, days, weeks, you never knew how long it would last. I was tired to my soul of having my very existence erased from my marriage because of some real or imagined slight or mistake. But one thing for sure was that the silence wouldn't end until I apologized and made things right. Apologized for nothing. Yet in my husband's eyes it was my fault and it was my job to fix it. Always. This time, however, I decided to ride it out and see what would happen. How would it play out if I made him apologize for once? I had never tried this and my curiosity was getting the best of me. I was done with having my self-esteem, my self-worth, my very identity as a living person held hostage by a man-child who enjoyed the power and control he held over my life. This particular episode of silence had lasted a week. I have no recollection of what prompted it, but it was usually a matter of me not paying enough attention to him, or not performing to his standards as a dutiful and respectful wife and servant. Not giving him my undivided attention or making him feel unimportant and disrespected was guaranteed to prompt silence.

It was in the fall, as I can remember being at a Halloween party with my family and he wasn't speaking to me. It was rather awkward and embarrassing, but what he was doing wasn't openly obvious to those around us. I was trying to make us appear as a "normal" family at the Halloween event, and the facade was working. No one in attendance suspected that my husband hadn't spoken to me in a week. We were playing the part of the all American family. We had all learned to become good actors; perfect on the outside. Returning home from the party, the facade faded and it was obvious that my husband was getting angrier by the minute with my refusal to apologize for whatever I had done, real or imagined.

I had taken to sleeping on the sofa because even being in the same room with him was difficult due to the awkwardness of being invisible. Imagine sharing a bed with someone and acting like they didn't exist? The next evening after the party he apparently decided that he'd had enough. He simply couldn't believe I hadn't yet caved to his authority, as I always did. His go to consequence that had always worked because it crumbled my self-esteem like a sand castle against high tide wasn't working this time. He must have felt like Oz when Dorothy pulled back the curtain and discovered his power was a fraud. He decided to switch tactics to the one I could not withstand.

Rather than make amends for once, he decided fear and intimidation would be the best route. It was his favorite route because he knew in his mind he had all the power. I was settling in on the sofa for the night, and I thought he had already gone to bed. I was then surprised when he emerged from the master bedroom fully dressed as if he was going somewhere. I asked him what he was doing even though I expected no verbal answer. I expected silence because that was his tool of emotional torture. But then he did something that let me know without a doubt that he was done being silent. He looked at me, then reached inside a lightweight jacket he was wearing and pulled out a handgun. I froze. Any thoughts I had about standing my ground evaporated in an instant. He opened the chamber to show me that there were in fact bullets inside. It was loaded.

I felt like a cold, wet blanket had just been draped across my shoulders and I got a queasy feeling in my stomach. Any feelings I had of bravery and strength disappeared like fog in the sun. The fear that streaked up my spine put all my senses into panic mode. He was no longer avoiding me, and he had my entire attention. My eyes were fixated on the handgun. He told me he was leaving the house to go kill himself because he was tired of dealing with me and my seeming lack of respect. I wasn't focused enough on him, and he needed to feel more important, more cherished, and I wasn't doing my job. I was making him miserable in public, at home, in the bedroom. He was going to end his life and it was all my fault. This made perfect and logical sense to him.

He left the house, and I went numb. I had absolutely no idea what to do. He had driven away with a loaded handgun and I had no idea where he was going. As a woman who had never dealt with this kind of thing before, I did not know then that this was a means to control me; to make me take the blame for a decision he had made, which was all for show. It was another form of manipulation to make me step in line and give into his control. I just didn't recognize it because at the time such a ploy was unfathomable to me.

My mind raced with what to do. Should I get help? Should I call 911? I was experiencing that all too familiar panic. My heart was racing, I was breaking out into a cold sweat and my hands were shaking. His plan was working, as he knew it would. If I tell anyone and he finds out he will be even more angry, especially if the police show up at our house. He could not have this kind of thing going public, not in the societal and business circles in which he moved. It would reveal a side of him he chose to keep hidden. A side of him that I helped to keep hidden. I was in a dilemma pacing through the house, weighing my options.

I considered that maybe I should do nothing. This was on him; his idea, his insane reaction. This thought didn't last long though. His plan was working and I was now in damage control mode to save him, and just like he would want, I began feeling guilty. I couldn't let him do this. I couldn't be held responsible for this. If only I had just apologized, been a better wife, given in when I should have...I had to stop him, but how? I had the phone in my hand as I paced through the house, trying to decide who to call. Maybe I should just call him? I had no idea what to do and the uncertainty of it all was almost too much for me to handle. I was starting to crack.

Fortunately I didn't have to wait long for an answer. Thirty minutes later my husband returned. I was actually overwhelmed with relief that he hadn't killed himself. I still didn't know it was just a ploy for control. This bit of drama was done to deliberately terrorize me and make me so emotionally unstable with fear and desperation that I would do whatever he said. I was so emotionally wrecked that I was totally in his power. And he knew it. He was still in possession of his loaded gun. It was there not to instill the fear of desperation from the loss of him, it now had a new purpose; to instill fear to demand compliance. My husband told me he had written something down and that he wanted me to read it while he recorded me on video. I had no idea what he was talking about. My mind was a spinning torrent of confusion and near insanity. I was just relieved that he in fact hadn't ended his life. I was willing to do just about anything to keep the peace at this moment, and that was the plan. Drive me to the breaking point to destroy my will. The gun was just there to make sure I didn't decide to regrow my backbone.

My husband handed me his written note and I stood in our master bedroom and read this one paragraph statement while he video recorded me with his phone. I looked like a hostage in a terrorist video, reading my statement to the nation. The paragraph detailed what a terrible wife I had been to him. It entailed how I didn't pay enough attention to him and his needs. I was made to admit what a poor excuse for a person I was. That I was ashamed of myself for being such an inadequate wife and that I was extremely selfish. It was a hate letter to myself, written by him, and I willingly read the words just wanting this event to be over. I was going to block it out of my mind if I could just manage to survive the next few minutes, and so I read. As I was reading, I was so emotionally disconnected from reality by the psychological onslaught of his "suicide attempt," that I could have confessed to anything written in his letter.

After I finished reading my "confession" he clicked off his phone. He informed me if I didn't "change" he would send this video recording to every person that we knew. My friends, my family, etc. He would use it to cause great humiliation for me. Everyone would know what a terrible wife and person I was. I had confessed to these charges on video, after all. Of course, no one would be able to see the gun behind the camera. No one could refute my words. I willingly incriminated myself. Had I just been blackmailed by my own husband? What had I just taken part in and gotten myself into? It didn't matter. It was over and he won. He was happy again. He was back in control, absolute control. I was degraded, insecure, scared and humiliated. He had me just where he wanted me, knew exactly how to break me, and proved I was an easy target for manipulation. Now I had the threat of this video hanging over me. I feared it more than the gun. He could use this video as leverage to control me. Now his life could return to normal. The silent treatment would be over and our happy family facade would begin again. He had gotten his apology, even though it had taken a sham suicide attempt, a near nervous breakdown, a forced confession and a loaded gun to make it happen.

Interestingly enough, this blackmail incident was never discussed or referred to again in our house. We could not have this getting out. It would ruin him. He treated it, instead, as if it had never happened. And he had the threat of the video to keep my silence and keep me from bringing the incident to light. I had my own personal sword over me and he held the thread. There were no apologies from him, no remorse, nothing. The next day it was like this incident had never happened. I managed to block it from my mind and deny to myself that it had in fact happened. I tucked it away with all of my other traumatic memories. He had shown to what lengths he would go to control me. If I didn't focus on it, I thought, then it will seem like nothing more than a bad dream. I was good at this tactic; a non-remembering of events. It was the easiest way to deal with the trauma that he was inflicting on me. I would tell myself whatever lie I needed to survive. I had to keep going, to keep up the facade of a normal life. Denial became the everyday way to live in my marriage.

You may ask what happened to the video. That's the million dollar question. To this day no one but my husband knows the location of this video or if it even still exists. This incident of blackmail was swept under the rug, like so many other incidents, never to be discussed again for years, with anyone, and I helped keep it that way. I was a good and obedient wife, after all.

The Narcissist's Prayer

That didn't happen.

And if it did, it wasn't that bad.

And if it was, it's not a big deal.

And if it is, that's not my fault.

And if it was, I didn't mean it.

And if I did, you deserved it.

15

Stockholm Syndrome

Many years into my marriage my parents began to voice some concerns. They were uncomfortable with the level of control they were witnessing. My husband's constant orders, his demeaning way of speaking to me and his total lack of empathy made them question my well being. They had even witnessed him throwing objects through the air in fits of rage. They spoke to me about it, curious to know what my thoughts were. I didn't want to hear it. I defended him. Always. "He's under a lot of stress. He works so hard. He's not usually like this." And so on and so on. I was helping him maintain his false persona. What else was I supposed to do? It's all I knew. I knew just how to take the blame, defend him at all costs and make sure his reputation was never marred. The protection of his reputation was essentially my job, and it was a full time job. It was my career. I managed to convince my parents in these early years that I was completely happy in my marriage, and they were at a loss to help. They didn't want to impede upon my contentedness so they just watched from afar and discussed amongst themselves. They saw plenty of good times, too, and they did see me happy. But I was both unknowingly and knowingly concealing a lot about the real dynamic of my relationship. I was slowly slipping into a fog. The abuse was unceasing, and my mindset became more and more clouded. I didn't realize at the time, but I was becoming trauma bonded. I was bonded to and dependent upon my abuser. And trauma bonds aren't easily broken.

Victims of narcissistic abuse often feel there is no hope for escape and no other options, so they try to fit in and adapt to their abuse in order to survive. Abuse becomes a way of life and ultimately the narcissist creates a voluntary victim. This type of dynamic is referred to as Stockholm Syndrome, a psychological manipulation tactic where hostages develop a bond with their captors. The term Stockholm Syndrome was first used in 1973 when four individuals were taken hostage during a bank robbery in Stockholm, Sweden. The perpetrator, armed with a submachine gun, held the hostages for six days inside one of the bank vaults. At the end of the six days, the hostages were safely released. To the surprise of authorities, none of the victims would testify against their captor. Instead, the hostages began a campaign to raise money for their captor's defense. This type of behavior, this act of protecting the abuser, is also referred to as trauma bonding.

Victims of narcissistic abuse become dependent on their

abusers due to a power imbalance. Oftentimes the abuser has power over the finances. They may hold physical power. And they hold power over the mind. Gaslighting. Abusers will say things like, "That never happened. You're remembering it all wrong. It wasn't really that bad." The victim begins to question their memory. Maybe it isn't all that bad? Maybe my memory is failing me? All the while, the trauma bond grows more and more solid. Victims will fixate on the "good days," finding all sorts of excuses for the abuse. They become incapable of seeing the red flags. Defend the abuser, deny the abuse, display persistent loyalty, and don't listen to anyone who tries to tell you differently. Effective trauma bonds generally involve five stages.

The first stage is the love bombing stage. The abuser overwhelms the victim with love and attention, making the victim feel like the most important person in the world. During this stage the victim becomes convinced that the abuser is actually a good person who has their best interest at heart. Trust is built through love bombing and the victim feels secure in the relationship.

Once the victim is completely trusting of the abuser, it is time for the abuser to start the criticism stage. During this time the victim's qualities are micro-managed and completely picked apart. My husband was great at this, even going as far as making lists of all the things I needed to change in order to better myself and make him happier. He criticized and critiqued everything I did, and that trust that I was building in him would slowly begin to crumble.

During the next stage the victim begins to give up, resigning to the fact that the abuser's behavior isn't going to change. At this stage of hopelessness the victim will often do anything to avoid conflict with the abuser. I most often used the "fawn" response, which is a trauma response that is typical of "people pleasers." I found it easiest to just keep my husband happy in order to avoid catastrophic tantrums.

The next stage involves the victim's loss of self. During this stage, I would reach a state of hopelessness which made me lose interest in activities that I previously enjoyed. I would find myself in a depressive state. Victims in this stage often feel sluggish with low energy. I would often find it hard to get out of bed, feeling very unmotivated to begin my day. Some victims in this stage may even feel a suicide ideation, as the loss of self can cause such a dark descent into depression.

The last stage of the trauma bond cycle is the cooling off stage. After the abuser pushes the victim to their breaking point, they may ease off. Ease off of the criticism and manipulation. During this stage the abuser may fake some remorse and may even fake an apology. This behavior will leave the victim feeling relieved and looking forward to the love bombing stage that will surely follow. For a short time it feels like life might be okay again. This cycle of love bombing, abuse and recovery becomes strangely addictive, and it creates a trauma bond that is strong and durable.

As my marriage progressed, I was becoming weaker and more submissive while my husband became more powerful and controlling. I was conditioned to continually forgive his behavior. Forgive and forget. And as the trauma bond strengthened, the idea of leaving my marriage became more and more unrealistic. I was stuck. I could never make it on my own, I thought, and I didn't have the strength to actually make a break. So, I made the best of it and tried to focus on the positive. I was unknowingly a victim of Stockholm Syndrome, trauma bonded to my abuser.

NINE SIGNS OF A TRAUMA BOND

1. The relationship gets too serious too quickly.

My relationship with my husband had progressed rather quickly. We began talking about marriage very shortly into our courtship, and we ultimately married at a young age. Narcissists like to hook you early. The quicker they can gain your loyalty, the quicker the mask can come off and they can begin controlling your behavior.

2. You begin losing touch with family and friends.

While I never actually lost touch with my friends and family, my husband was very jealous of these people and took issue with how much time I spent with my parents and or talking to them on the phone. He wanted my undivided attention after all. Narcissists see friends and family as an ultimate threat to their control.

3. You compromise yourself for the sake of the relationship.

I did this nearly every day, or at least it felt like I did. I compromised my happiness to make sure he stayed happy. It was much easier to keep him happy and un-triggered than the alternative. When he was angry, life was miserable. So, I lowered my expectations and only required minimal happiness. Life was easier this way.

4. You set boundaries that are consistently crossed.

My boundaries didn't exist. I had none. Any boundary that I had early on had not only been crossed, but it had been broken. My husband's control superseded any boundary that even remotely existed. Perhaps the things that narcissists hate most are boundaries.

5. You are afraid to speak out after you have been mistreated.

I would never speak out about my husband's mistreatment of me, at least not in the beginning. My goal was to cover for him at all costs, making our family seem normal. I craved normalcy and protecting his false persona was the best way to achieve this. Narcissists are adept at making their victims afraid to unmask them. The victim learns to be the protector of the mask.

6. You blame yourself for everything.

My husband blamed me for every single thing that went wrong in our relationship, even if it was his fault. This became a way of life for us and I began accepting all of the blame early on. Over time I actually believed I was to blame for everything and guilt was a common emotion that I felt. Narcissists oftentimes seek out those whom they feel can be easily guilted into accepting all of the blame.

7. You feel lost without them.

I became convinced in our early years of marriage that I wasn't capable of sustaining a comfortable life without my husband. He was the smartest one, the most successful one, the one who took care of finances, and I didn't have the knowledge, according to him, to ever sustain on my own. By making the victim feel helpless, the narcissist gains more control and more security that the victim will never betray them.

8. You make up excuses for their abuse.

I didn't want anyone to see my husband as an abuser. So I convinced myself he wasn't an abuser. I denied the abuse for years and years refusing to see myself as any kind of victim. Being a victim was embarrassing to me and it was easier to make up excuses for his behavior than to suffer the embarrassment of being married to an abuser.

9. You feel as if you're running in circles.

I felt spread too thin most all of the time. There wasn't enough of me to go around. The kids needed me, my husband demanded me and there weren't enough hours in the day to take care of pets, the house, the kids and my demanding husband who wanted all attention on him. Running in circles was how I lived, and it was exhausting.

16

The Teen Years

As our children moved into their teenage years more tension arose in our house. Teenagers are challenging in their own right, but pairing teenagers with a narcissistic father was a recipe for disaster. My husband wanted peace and perfection all the time. There was no room for chaos, arguing or fighting amongst the kids. He didn't deserve anything less than a picture perfect life. Any time there was conflict between our teens, my husband blamed me. I was a terrible parent. I wasn't doing my job to control the kids. Everything and everybody in my husband's world needed to be controlled, after all, and kids being kids just wasn't acceptable.

It was a day to day juggling act. Keep the kids happy and peaceful, all while paying enough attention to my husband. There literally wasn't enough of me to go around. I was being spread way too thin. I found that when my kids had friends over life ran smoother. It kept the kids out of each other's hair and another person in the house forced my husband to be on better behavior. After all, he loved to make good impressions. The more people I could put around us, the easier it was to keep the peace, and peace was what I yearned for.

Around the age of 13, my daughter began to form some strong opinions about her father. She became more in tune to his abusively controlling behaviors and she became less and less impressed with his character. She saw his angry outbursts, his toddler style temper tantrums and his erratic and unpredictable behavior, and this caused her to begin withdrawing from him. Their relationship was one of tension, and I was caught in the middle. My husband would schedule "meetings" with me to discuss this issue. In his twisted mind, I was creating the tension between him and his teen daughter. I was commiserating with her instead of building him up. We had lots of meetings on this very subject, and he would make me promise to craft ways to improve their relationship. He wasn't going to improve their father daughter bond, or lack thereof. That was my job. I was expected to make it happen. "Come up with a plan," he would say. He wanted me to think of fun activities for them to engage in together. He truly did want to build a bond with his daughter but had no clue where to start. I needed to solve this problem for him because I was the one who had caused it, according to him. I was letting their relationship deteriorate. Me, not him. That's how it always was. It was never him, and this was the very attitude that was slowly turning my daughter against her father.

Tension became a way of life in our house, and we all learned how to live in a tense environment. But sometimes everyone in the family was happy and everyone would get along. During these times we made some good memories, like a normal family should. We laughed, we enjoyed each other's company, we acted silly and we seemed like a picture perfect unit. At times we felt normal. But not all of the time. Not nearly enough. There was always the elephant in the room. The narcissistic father and husband.

Our son, having been diagnosed at a young age with a mild form of high functioning autism, saw some challenges in his preteen years. Daily life was a little more difficult for him. My son had trouble regulating his emotions and stressful situations could feel like the end of the world for him. He could become easily upset and cry for hours over seemingly small things. His nervous system was immature and he required careful handling. Of course my husband was of no help during this phase of our lives. He didn't deserve this challenge. His only contribution, which he was proud to say, was paying for the various occupational therapy sessions and social skills classes that I enrolled our son into. As for the difficult days, the meltdowns and all that goes along with mild autism, I was on my own. The meltdowns and crying fits would distress my husband so much, and I couldn't deal with two meltdowns. One was enough. My husband didn't know how to support me through this stage of our lives, nor did he have any interest in trying to support me. He would simply leave the house, and I would be left to calm our son by myself. This became normal. If my son was having a difficult day I had to do my best to keep him separated from my husband, trying to maintain that Norman Rockwell facade simply for my husband's benefit. I became quite literally a single parent. My husband was present for the happy times, and only the happy times. He deserved no less. He was better than us, more deserving than us, and he couldn't stoop so low as to be a parent on the difficult days. That was my job and my job alone.

17

Anger Management

My husband's tantrums got more and more emphatic as the years went on. When life didn't go his way he reacted, and his reactions were having a greater effect on the family with each passing day. My anxiety was rising and panic attacks became a way of life for me. The racing heartbeat, sweaty palms, shortness of breath, it was a miserable feeling. I had so much on my plate and I wasn't sure how much longer I could endure my lifestyle. After another particularly erratic fit by my husband, which involved yelling, slamming doors and items being thrown into the floor, I decided to finally put my foot down. Putting my foot down wasn't something I was well versed in, but I decided to give it my best shot. I approached my husband in his home office to have a talk with him. I told him point blank that he had an anger management problem. I then told him that he needed to get himself into therapy or he would lose his family. I explained that the kids were being affected by his behavior and that he was creating too much anxiety for everyone in the house. We couldn't possibly continue to live in this house together unless his behavior changed quickly and dramatically.

I had taken a risk, and I didn't know how my husband would react. I feared this direct approach might send him into another tantrum state, but to my surprise he readily agreed with me. The idea of therapy was intriguing to him and he was more than willing to give it a try. He spent some time researching therapists in our area and found a highly qualified man that he thought looked promising. He made an initial appointment and went to his first intake session. He then proceeded to go to sessions each week for one hour. Things seemed normal at home, at least for the meantime. My husband seemed calmer and less triggered. Maybe these sessions were working. I thought this was surely a turning point in our marriage and in our family. I had found the magic potion- therapy. This would fix all of our problems and we could be ordinary. I was cautiously optimistic.

After about a month of therapy, my husband arranged for me to go to a session with him. He had said very little about his sessions and I hadn't wanted to pry too much. Fingers crossed, life was going well and I didn't want to rock the boat. I was very curious to attend a session with him to find out what types of things the therapist was working on with my husband. Clearly, the curriculum was effective. When the day came for our appointment we entered the therapist's office and sat down on the sofa. I expected this man to explain my husband's anger management issues, why he was the way he was, and what was being done to try and help him. But this isn't how the session went. Not at all.

The therapist first explained to me that in his professional opinion my husband didn't have an anger management problem. He was just a little stressed due to his high level job. Overall, he was a pretty laid back, calm guy. No issues were noted. I was in complete shock. I couldn't believe what I was hearing. It didn't even occur to me at the time to argue with this gentleman or tell him the things that were going on in my home- the rage, the fits, the verbal abuse, and so on. Instead, I believed this man. After all, he had a fancy framed diploma hanging on his wall. He must know more than me about these types of things. I began gaslighting myself. I had been over reacting, I was too sensitive and I had been blowing my husband's behavior completely out of context. I was feeling foolish. I had sent my husband to therapy and he didn't even have a condition that warranted treatment. The professional psychologist had just sat in front of me and said that my husband did not have a problem with anger. He was completely and utterly normal.

After the initial shock from the therapist, I received another shock. I wasn't prepared for this bit of information that was about to come my way. I wasn't completely sure why I had been summoned to this therapy session in the first place, but I was about to find out. The therapist informed me that after counseling my husband through several sessions, it had been divulged that my husband had suffered severe trauma as a young child.

After 20 plus year of marriage this was the first time I was hearing this information. Why hadn't he ever mentioned this before? My husband simply said he just put it in the back of his mind and never spoke of it. But he was speaking now. I felt terrible for him, naturally, and I was completely sidelined by the fact that the conversation had diverged from an anger management problem that apparently didn't exist, to a conversation about my husband being abused as a child. My head was spinning. I wasn't prepared for any of this, and when we left the therapist's office I had very little to say. This was going to take some time to process.

By the next day my husband's angry attitude had returned. He was appalled that I hadn't been more sympathetic toward him after finding out about his past. I honestly wasn't sure what I was supposed to do, and I verbalized this to him. I told him I was sorry he had endured a difficult childhood. No child deserves trauma in their upbringing. I wasn't sure what else I was supposed to say. This wasn't a situation I was prepared to deal with. My response, or lack thereof, infuriated my husband. He told me I could "fix" this past trauma he had experienced if I would just respond appropriately. I was beyond confused, partly because I was dealing with my own trauma that he was causing me. There was too much trauma in this house, past and present, and I just didn't know how to address any of it. And then my husband made a statement to me that chilled me to the bone. "You haven't given me enough sympathy for what I went through as a kid, and you refuse to meet my emotional needs; that makes you just as bad of a person as my perpetrator." What? I thought surely I had heard him wrong. I asked him to clarify and he did. Yes, in fact, he viewed me as evil as his abuser who had stolen his innocence as a young child. In his eyes, my unwillingness to meet his emotional needs made me equal to a child abuser.. And he meant and felt every word he had just spoken.

The whole therapist endeavor had left me with more questions than answers. At the end of the day I was told that I had misdiagnosed my husband's anger and that I was effectively evil. My husband had fooled the therapist, putting on a compelling show and then blindsided me with bombshell information about his past. And now I was seemingly the one with the issue. Everything I had been working toward had just been derailed. So much for therapy. My problems were mounting instead of abating.

18

Generational Trauma

When life was good it was good, and when it was bad it was horrendous. There were many days that I wanted to leave. I felt that I could raise these two children more effectively if my husband wasn't in the same house. I dreamt of the three of us, me, my son and my daughter, living in a home by ourselves. Just the three of us doing life together in peace. This dream didn't become a reality, though because I didn't want to be the one to break up the family. I didn't want to share custody of my kids.

I didn't want to share my kids on holidays. I couldn't think of anything worse, at least not at that time. So I stayed for the kids. I let my kids witness toxic behaviors, all while trying to make it look normal. Kids are wiser than we think though, and kids are observant. They may not know how to process the trauma they are witnessing and experiencing, but they most definitely can feel it. My daughter was feeling her trauma to the point that she began self harming. The pain she would cause to herself through cutting was a way to numb the emotional pain she was feeling. If she could cause more pain to her skin, then the emotional pain would become more manageable and less present. She was in a miserable place while trying to navigate her teenage years. She was seeking relief from her problems, and I was helpless.

I was completely overwhelmed with everything going on in our household. My kids were struggling with their separate issues and my family was falling apart. The emotional abuse was almost intolerable for me and my kids were suffering. I can best describe these years using a metaphor of a stained glass window. A beautiful, colorful scene. It was as if everyday a rock would be thrown into this window and it would shatter, colored glass sprinkled everywhere. I would spend my days picking up the tiny pieces and trying to reassemble them into that beautiful scene once again. I would tape the pieces together, and while it never looked like it should, it was still a beautiful piece of stained glass with some small visible scarring. But then the next day another rock would be hurled. And just like the day before, that stained glass picture would shatter, this time in even more pieces. And once again I would spend the day trying to make the pieces fit back together.

This was how we lived for far too many years. I was remaining in this life seemingly for the sake of the kids. I had to choose between a broken home and a toxic home and by choosing the "unbroken" home I thought I was making a smart decision. I was keeping my family together. I was being a good mom, or so I thought. However, I would learn later that this was not the smartest thing I could have chosen to do.

Generational Trauma. This is the idea that trauma can be passed down through generations. Generational trauma can be set in motion when traumatic experiences create psychological and physical symptoms in an individual. These symptoms, like depression and anxiety, can then affect the individual's future relationships and family, making it harder to trust others, harder to form healthy bonds, and thus causing the trauma to literally trickle down through future generations. Children learn a lot from observing their parents. Unfortunately, in a toxic home children can learn toxic behaviors. Without proper therapy these behaviors can continue into adulthood, and thus begins a vicious cycle. The trauma from being in an abusive home can have shattering effects, not just on our generation but generations to follow. Children, grandchildren, great grandchildren. All of these people can potentially be affected by the trauma that is happening today. This information sent chills down my spine. All this time I thought I was doing what was best for my kids by preserving a family unit. Doing the "right" thing. In fact, I was damaging not only my children but potentially my future grandchildren and so on down the line. This was not my intention, and it would be the source of much guilt in the following years. Staying for the kids is not always the best decision, as I now know. There is simply too much at stake when dealing with damage to one's mental health. Trauma is real, and like a virus, it can unfortunately be contagious.

19

Coercive Control

Another common trait seen in many narcissistic relationships is coercive control. Coercive control is basically an ongoing and increasing pattern of severe manipulation that can create major psychological damage to the victim. Narcissists will use intimidation and humiliation to coercively control. They may begin to dictate what their victim eats, how they sleep or what they wear, micromanaging all aspects of their victim's life. They will also guilt-trip to gain control and satisfy their desires. My husband was the master of guilt-tripping. He knew just how to make me feel like the worst person on earth, and as a result he could convince me of almost anything, as I believed he was the better person in the relationship. As a business man, he loved to hold meetings and would often schedule meetings with me. We would meet to discuss my perceived "issues." I needed to learn how to prioritize my time, get my priorities in line, and make him the most important person on earth. Ever the visual learner, he loved to create spreadsheets, graphs and lists which aided him in accomplishing his goals. It was clear to me that I was slowly becoming a spreadsheet. As the years dragged on I was becoming less and less of a person. I was instead an object that he owned. I was merely a list, an obstacle to conquer, and enough graphs and charts would surely be able to fix me.

About 20 years into my marriage my husband's coercive control and micro managing of my life was at an all time high. I was slowly deteriorating under the constant pressure and scrutiny. I needed to find an outlet for my stress or I was going to have a mental breakdown. I could feel it coming. I have a creative gene and I had always been curious about fiber arts, namely crochet. One day out of the blue I decided to teach myself to crochet. I struggled at first and found it frustrating. I sure didn't need any more frustration in my life. But I was determined and this seemed like a great stress management tool if I could ever master the art.

I enrolled in an afternoon class at a local craft store. The class began with five students. Two hours later four of the students were gone, one in tears, saying it was too frustrating. I was the only one left along with the instructor. By the time I left the craft store I was hooked, no pun intended. I crocheted every time I got a free second. I put all of my frustrations and stress into this intricate craft and found it to be the best therapy I could ever experience. With my crochet hook in hand and a skein of yarn I could forget all my problems and completely decompress while using repetitive motions to craft my creations. I stayed up late into the night most nights working on small stuffed toys and whimsical projects. My husband was not impressed. He saw it as a waste of time and often told me it was embarrassing. "Don't let anyone see you doing that," he would often say. "That's only for old people. You don't need a hobby anyway. You have other responsibilities that are more important." And by "more important" he was referring to himself. But to his dismay I didn't stop, and a year later my hobby grew into a small business.

The last thing my husband wanted me to do was have an interest or activity that didn't involve him. So during one of our meetings he informed me that my earnings from my small crochet business were not worthy of my time. "I make more money in five minutes than you make in a month," he told me. His math was correct. He made a lot of money in his high powered executive job. I made side income with my hobby job. It was a fact. He decided that the time I spent on my business was effectively wasted time. The pay out wasn't great enough. Therefore, by his logic, I should shut down my business, pack it up and forget it. My time was better spent with him. If I quit my small business I could devote myself to bettering our marriage, and in his mind it would be a better use of my time. My dollar per hour income with simply too low according to him. I shouldn't be wasting my life. I should be using this time to work on my shortcomings and improve our relationship.

Using his very effective guilt tripping techniques, he began to make progress, and I began to consider giving up my small business. In retrospect I'm not sure if I was serious, or if I was curious about his reaction, but I eventually told my husband that I was shutting down my business. I was giving up my crafting hobby that I loved. A hobby that was perhaps my biggest stress reliever. I stated that I would sell what was left of my inventory and my hobby would be a thing of the past. Curious, I wanted to see what his reaction would be. He said very little, but appeared to nod with approval. He certainly wasn't trying to convince me otherwise. He was likely proud that I had taken his advice. I let it ride for a couple of days to see what would happen. I took no action to shut down anything, but instead simply closed the door of my craft room and made him think I was on board with his flawed logic.

My husband was the happiest I had seen him in months. There was a marked difference in his attitude, and I wasn't sure what to make of it. A few days later he presented me with a surprise- a gift certificate for a one hour massage. He said it was just a "just because" gift. The truth was, he had bought me a gift because I had agreed to give up my small hobby business. He had won, and he wanted to show his immense gratitude. He felt that I deserved a much needed massage. I gladly accepted the gift card and it then became clear to me what he was doing. He was pushing me as far as he could. He had just made me agree to give up my hobby and business. He was thrilled. He had exerted his control, and it had been effective once again, or so he thought.

I booked my massage and thoroughly enjoyed it, but never

actually held up my end of the bargain. My business continued, and my husband's anger crept back in once he realized his mission hadn't exactly been fulfilled. He had gone out of his way to purchase a gift card for me. He had spent a hundred dollars after all, and he wasn't being rewarded for his efforts. Crafting had won and he had lost. I was seemingly getting a little braver with age, and beginning to push back ever so slightly. I was beginning to test my limits with him, and I was attempting to take back a minuscule amount of my power that had been stolen from me in the early days of marriage.

5 SIGNS OF COERCIVE CONTROL

Isolating you from your support system

While I wasn't actually isolated, my husband took note of how much time I would spend talking to friends or family or interacting with them. He didn't want anyone to get more attention than he did. While he could talk to a friend or a family member for an hour on the phone, I was chastised if I did such a thing. Narcissists don't want you to have outside support. They see this as a threat and it diminishes their control over you.

Monitoring your activity throughout the day

My husband would occasionally check my phone to see how much time I had spent perusing social media. He kept close tabs on me through a tracking app, but claimed this was for safety reasons. Of course tracking apps are a great safety feature but at times his use of these apps bordered on stalking. Narcissists like to know your every move. It's just another means of total control.

Denying your autonomy

My husband didn't like the idea of me having my "own life", and he preferred for me to not work. While I held occasional, small part time jobs throughout our marriage, my undivided attention was more valuable to him than any income I could make.

Gaslighting

I was gaslighted from day one of our marriage. My husband set the narrative. I willingly followed along to the point that I eventually began gaslighting myself, convincing myself that I was too sensitive and that my perception must be warped.

Restricting your access to money

Throughout our marriage we had many bank accounts, although I only had access to our basic checking account. I had no access to the large accounts nor did I have a credit card. I only possessed a debit card and that limited me to only the funds that were in our checking. Retaining a divorce attorney or the like wouldn't have been attainable to me without seeking outside help. My husband's control of the finances also controlled me.

20

A Walk

While my marriage saw many good days and good times, mind boggling narcissistic behavior could appear out of nowhere with no warning whatsoever. Something so simple like a difference in opinion or an insignificant event could trigger anger or rage faster than the snap of a finger. I was a victim of trauma, though I didn't realize it, and I had learned over the years to anticipate my husband's moods. I was in tune to the tone of his voice, the look in this eyes, and his manner of walking. All of these things could clue me in to a possible upcoming narcissistic rage. Like a tornado watcher, I learned to study the winds so I could predict when the disturbance was coming. I could divert his attention and do damage control before the damage occurred. But sometimes, even with all of my hyper vigilance, I missed the storm warnings.

One particular day my husband decided he was going on an afternoon walk and wanted me to come along. Most days when he walked I would accompany him. But on this day I declined. I was suffering from a lot of chronic pain, that I would later understand was due to the high levels of stress I was living under. I told him that I wasn't feeling great and that I would prefer to sit this one out and stay home. My husband turned and left the room, clearly upset by my response. It wasn't what he wanted to hear. To my surprise, that response actually precipitated one week of anger. My husband wavered between the silent treatment and verbal abuse for the next few days. He informed me that I was not "fun" anymore, and that he couldn't foresee a happy future with me if I refused to share his interests. This was all because I declined to go on a walk with him. A simple, afternoon walk. It made no sense to me, but it made perfect sense to him. I had refused to spend time with him, and he couldn't believe it. He saw my actions as a rejection. I had rejected his idea of fun. I had robbed him of entertainment. I had made him feel small. In his mind he had been wronged by his wife once again.

My husband believed my refusal to walk with him on that day was cruel treatment, and that I should feel terribly guilty about declining to accompany him on his lovely afternoon stroll. The truth was, I enjoyed time alone because I rarely got it. And any time he was out of the house was a chance for me to feel like I could breathe again. That feeling of suffocation evaporated from the room for the brief time that he would be out of my presence. So while I in fact didn't feel like walking that day,

I also needed a break. I needed a break from his overbearing presence. I needed to breathe, if only for a short time. My husband's demands were getting more and more ridiculous. It was almost as if he was saying, "Share my interests, or else!" If an afternoon walk could trigger such a reaction from him, I shuddered to think what my future held. Over time I began to feel like my time was no longer mine, my space was no longer mine, and my life was no longer mine. I was literally suffocating under the pressure of my husband's unattainable demands.

21

Sleep Deprivation

The funny thing about narcissism is that it doesn't get better. It only gets worse. And each year of my marriage was a little bit worse than the last. When my husband reached his 50th birthday his sense of entitlement and his level of coercive control was markedly more extreme. We were about 26 years into our marriage, and life was becoming unbearable. I was finding that coping with an aging narcissist was draining me both physically and emotionally. I was experiencing chronic pain and anxiety attacks almost daily. The pain became intense enough that I was tested for an array of autoimmune diseases, including rheumatoid arthritis. Fortunately I got negative results, but my pain wasn't subsiding. I was expected to devote 24/7 to him, and I was completely exhausted. His tone grew more and more condescending and I, according to him, was becoming more and more incapable.

He would bark out orders to me, and as exhausted and worn out as I was, I would try to comply. Pleasing him became an impossible task, and it was getting more impossible with each passing year. No matter what, everything I did was wrong. Not good enough. I was almost good enough, but I couldn't quite make it into the "good enough" category. "What's wrong with you?" he would often ask. "Why can't you follow simple instructions? Are you stupid?" And I couldn't even think about watching a tv show or having some "me" time, reading a book, or browsing social media. It wasn't worth the fall out. If he was awake, life was all about him. He even went so far as confiscating my phone and checking my usage to see how many minutes I had been reading social media posts. He would then add these minutes to the amount of time that I spent watching a short television show. He would then calculate the total number of minutes I "wasted," not spending them with him. My life became one giant math equation. I began to crave the times that my husband was asleep. Once he had gone to sleep for the night I could watch my tv shows, read my books and just enjoy some peace without scrutiny. While I managed to squeeze in this "me" time in the dark hours of the night, this life was not sustainable, and I knew it. I was sleeping an average of 3 hours a night and exhausting myself all day long to make sure I didn't trigger him. Something had to give...soon.

Perhaps one of the most bizarre behaviors I witnessed in my narcissistic husband was his use of sleep deprivation as means of control. I would eventually learn that this is a common tactic used by these types of people, and the reasons for their use of sleep deprivation are chilling. In my household it was common-place for my husband to be angry if I fell asleep before him. In his mind he worked harder and expended more energy through-out the day than I did, and if he wasn't tired then I shouldn't be either. And of course if I was asleep then I was of no use to him. I couldn't jump up to fix him a snack, bring him a drink, or watch a movie with him. My exhaustion was a sign of weakness according to him. But it was also a way for him to control me.

Being in a state of exhaustion keeps an individual in a fog-like state, making it harder to think straight. And if I'm not think-ing straight I'm more easy to manipulate. Sleep deprivation also causes memory fog or memory loss, both long and short term. And of course, this assists the narcissist with the gaslighting technique, making it easier to convince the victim that they are recalling events incorrectly. Depriving a victim of sleep gives power to the narcissist, and that's their number one goal. And I later learned that purposely depriving someone of sleep is actually a form of physical abuse.

Narcissists have a variety of ways they commonly use to create sleep deprivation. A favorite technique of my husband's was to start a serious conversation at bedtime, and a conversation with a narcissist is not your typical conversation. These monologues tend to be circular in nature, going around and around and around and lasting for hours. My husband's personal record for a "conversation" was 5 hours. He had important things to dis-cuss. We needed to talk about why I don't prioritize him, how I can be a better wife for him, how important he is, or all of the things he needs me to do for him tomorrow. And if I dare fall asleep or get too tired during this conversation, then I'm weak. I'm unworthy. "What is wrong with you? You get more than enough sleep. There is no reason in the world that you should be tired," he would say. Narcissists will also be careless when their victim is asleep, barging loudly into the room, turning on lights and slamming drawers. In true narcissistic fashion, they have no regard for their sleeping victim. If my husband woke me up it wasn't a big deal. I didn't need that much sleep anyway, according to him. And the next day he would have me just where he wanted me- exhausted and easily manipulated.

While my narcissistic husband didn't mind to deprive me of sleep, he was serious about his own sleep. He was important, after all. He needed a good night's rest so he could maintain his perception of perfection. Something that angered him greatly was being awoken from a peaceful slumber. On one particular Saturday night we had gone to sleep around 11:00 PM. It was the weekend, and my husband wasn't working the next day. He had the flexibility of sleeping in. But nonetheless, one must not dare disturb his coveted sleep schedule. So when one of our teens came into our room late in the night to ask for an extra blanket, my husband was rustled awake and he wasn't cheerful. I gladly got up and retrieved the needed blanket and then headed back to bed. This wasn't a big issue to me. It was the weekend after all. To my husband, however, it was a catastrophe.

After our child left our room my husband had a toddler style meltdown. How dare I let our child into our room to wake him up. He cannot be inconvenienced in this way. It's wasn't fair. His sleep is of the utmost importance, after all. So, not surprisingly, he announced to me that he was leaving. Was he leaving for an hour, a night, a week, or forever? Who knew? But one thing was for sure. He let me know that he absolutely couldn't live in this house with people waking him up. Sounds a bit extreme, but not to him. In fact, this sounded completely logical to him at 1:00 in the morning. He got out of bed and aggressively packed a bag. He packed clothes, shoes, cosmetics and everything he might need for an extended stay for wherever he would be journeying. He then started his car and peeled out of the driveway. When he was angry he wanted everyone to know. He threw his fits in grand fashion. I hoped this immature tantrum was finished, at least until morning. I had no idea where he was going. I was just relieved to see his taillights as he departed and to know that I wouldn't have to deal with him until at least the next day. But as usual, I was wrong.

About 20 minutes later my cell phone rang. It was him. "Are you awake?" "I am now," I replied. His response was, "Good." He proceeded to tell me that he would be calling my cell phone every 15 minutes for the remainder of the night to make sure I was awake. I was not allowed to sleep if he wasn't. Since he had been awoken then I should remain awake with him. And he let me know that I better answer my phone. I wanted to make sure he stayed gone, so I did just that- I answered my phone. I couldn't think of any other option. Every 15 minutes the phone rang. "Are you asleep?" he would ask. "No," I would reply. And this went on for hours. He was relishing in the fact that I was not getting sleep. If he doesn't sleep, no one does. And what I didn't realize at the time was that this insensitive act of his was actually a form of physical abuse. Even though he didn't use his hands, his sinister plan to keep me awake was abusing my body. And once again he felt in control, right where he liked to be.

My husband eventually retuned home in the wee hours of the morning. He was finally tired and he retreated to bed to get some much needed rest. His being home again put me on edge, and any hope of grabbing a few moments of sleep had just gone out the window. I moved to the couch, not wanting to be in the same room with him, but there would be no sleep coming for me. I was over-tired and tense and I knew it would take a day to unwind from the stressful night I had just endured. In those early morning hours I was feeling exhausted and frazzled and my mind was racing. My husband, however, was sleeping like a baby.

22

Late Night Escape

After the sleep deprivation incident with my husband, we didn't speak for about two weeks. It was awkward. We were living in the same house yet avoiding each other like the plague. I made it a point not to be in the same room with him. I tried to stay out of the house during the day when he was home. I ran errands that didn't need to be run, and I did a lot of unnecessary grocery shopping, taking lots of extra time to browse each aisle at the store. I felt relaxed and somewhat free when I was out and about. On most days I would pick up lunch at a sandwich shop and sit in my car in a parking lot, enjoying a nice peaceful meal. It was these little moments of solitude that kept me functional. But then it would be time to return home, and pulling my car back into the driveway stirred the worst feelings of hopelessness.

I began sleeping in an upstairs guest bedroom during this time of belittling silence, and my husband remained in the master bedroom. He was the master, after all. He couldn't be expected to abandon his throne. As the days of his childish behavior went on, my husband was becoming more and more angry. I could literally tell by the look in his eyes. It was a hollow, empty look with his eyes slightly squinted all the time. It was obvious to me that he was more angry than I had ever seen him in our marriage. Once again, I was refusing to apologize and make things right, and this wasn't acceptable to him. I refused to take the blame for whatever it was I had done. I really had no idea what I had done that could reap such a harsh reaction as the one I was receiving, and I wasn't sure that I cared. I was honestly enjoying the peacefulness of not having to deal with my husband. In retaliation he began making life in the house harder for me.

In the evenings he would retreat to the bedroom and lock the door. I couldn't get in to get clothes, makeup, or even my toothbrush. His door locking became routine and I started moving some of my things out of the bedroom and into the guest room where I was staying. This was getting beyond ridiculous and I had no idea where we were headed. I just knew that apparently I had a new bedroom, and I was perfectly okay with that. I then began to notice my husband taking bottles of wine into our master bedroom each night. This was not in character for him at all. He had never been a drinker for as long as I had known him. But now, suddenly, one or two bottles of wine were being confiscated from our butler pantry every night. It was clear that he was getting intoxicated behind that locked door of our bedroom. He was so angry and the idea of him being angry and drunk was a combination that frightened me.

On one particular night about, two weeks into our journey of silence, both of our kids were gone for the night at friends' houses and I was at home with my husband. I saw him stealthily steal away in our room with alcohol in hand at about 9 PM and I was immediately uncomfortable. I was in the house alone with him. He was going to get drunk and his anger toward me was ruminating with each passing day. My house didn't feel like the safest place to be that night, so I called my parents who lived about 10 minutes away. I explained the situation. They had been growing more and more uncomfortable with my husband's behavior, as they were beginning to see a side of him that they no longer recognized. They agreed that I shouldn't be in the house alone with him and my mom said she was coming over to pick me up. This is where it would get tricky, though.

I didn't want my husband to know I was leaving. He was angry enough and I didn't want to trigger him further. I was sure he was intoxicated by now. I went to the security panel that was farthest from the master bedroom and I disabled the door chime, hoping he wouldn't hear the buttons beeping. I was then able to leave out of a side door and close it quietly. I attempted to make my way down the driveway, avoiding the security cameras he had placed all around our property. I arranged for my mom to pick me up at the end of the street so he wouldn't catch a glimpse of any car lights. As I was walking down the dark street toward her car I couldn't believe myself. I was 48 years old, and I was sneaking out of my own house, walking down the street in the pitch dark to safety. This was stuff I had only read about in books and seen in thriller movies. This could not be real. My life was growing more insane with each passing day.

Safely at my parents' house I settled in for the night. I was exhausted and desperately needed a good night's sleep. Just as I was dozing off my phone dinged. It was a text from him. "Where are you?" I started to panic but then remembered I was at my parents' house. There was nothing he could do. I was safe. I told him exactly where I was. He told me that we needed to talk. It was urgent. I expressed to him that I was not returning that night and it would have to wait until morning. He kept repeating the phrase, "time is of the essence." I had no idea what he meant and still don't know why he chose this exact phrase, although he did love to cause alarm and this phrase sounded urgent. Nonetheless I agreed to return first thing in the morning to talk. I didn't know if it was safe, but morning felt safer than night for some reason. Perhaps he would be sober enough in the morning that he would actually be reasonable. I set my phone down and attempted to sleep, but no sleep came. I worried the entire night about how our talk would go in the morning. After several sleepless hours I returned home at 6:30AM to attend a meeting with my husband. I was hoping and praying that he was going to ask me for a divorce.

Upon retuning home I quickly discovered that my hopes would not come to fruition. My husband wanted to talk about how we could salvage this marriage. We sat in our master bedroom and he talked and he talked and he talked. I was being interrogated as though I was on trial for a heinous crime. Our bedroom had now become a courtroom and I was the defendant. "What is wrong with you? Why can't you have an emotional connection with me? What the hell is your problem," he exclaimed. He expected answers and I didn't have any. I didn't know why I felt nothing for him. I just didn't. I was growing more and more scared of him by the day and he was honestly the last person I wanted to be around, let alone have any kind of emotional connection with.

When all else failed and he couldn't get the answers he wanted he pulled out a new trump card. A new last resort. Religion. "You cannot call yourself a Christian if you don't honor your husband." I couldn't imagine where this was going. My minimally religious husband was now quoting the Bible like he was some kind of biblical scholar fresh out of seminary. He was literally preaching to me as though he had just stepped out of the 1950's. "I want you to admit to me that you're not a Christian. You can't be a Christian with the way you are acting toward me. I am your husband and wives are supposed to submit." I was really forming a track record here. I was apparently evil for not adequately sympathizing with his traumatic youth and now I was no longer a Christian because I wouldn't bow to him.

My husband's speech went for a grand total of 5 hours. I was captive in our room, listening to all the ways that I had wronged him for an exhaustive five whole hours. There was no exiting this conversation either. That would just incite more rage. It was safer to sit and listen to his intense rambling that was beginning to sound more and more sociopathic as the hours progressed. I was effectively a hostage. I was beyond exhausted, especially considering the fact that I hadn't slept the night before. His had been an interrogation meant to wear me down. This was his goal. After five hours I was wiling to say or agree to anything just to be set free from that room. I ultimately agreed to work on our relationship, whatever that meant. I really had no idea to what I had just agreed. I just needed the lecture to be over. I was slowly beginning to see that I was living in an un-sane home and that while I had agreed to try and restore this marriage I ultimately knew I couldn't continue living this way and retain my sanity.

23

A College Trip

As my marriage was falling apart, our oldest child was leaving for college. We were moving her 600 miles away to a new city. We would be taking her to college and then driving back home, diverting for a short vacation on the way. I was dreading making this trip with my husband. While we were now on speaking terms it was still tense. I had agreed to try and work things out with him, but I knew in my heart the abuse would not cease. We would be driving separate from my daughter and all I could think about were the implications of being trapped in a car with him for this trip. I thought of every way possible that I could avoid riding with him, but nothing seemed logical. I wasn't going to miss taking my daughter to college. This was a defining life moment, after all. So I had no choice but to take this journey with my narcissistic husband. As a passenger in a car, I knew there would be nowhere to go to escape his verbal abuse, which I was sure was on his agenda. I was afraid I would be stuck in a whirlwind of lectures, and that's just the position in which I would find myself. That is also the position that he wanted me in. I would be a captive audience to him. However, I was trying to be positive. I wanted to make the best of this trip. I thought just maybe it would work out better than I anticipated. I spent some time creating some Spotify playlists for us to listen to on the long car ride. I wanted to limit the verbal onslaught that I was sure he was planning, so I thought if we could enjoy some music together it would lessen the tension of the trip. My playlists never came into play on this journey, though. You see, my husband, too, had been working on his own playlist.

My husband had discovered a podcast he thought was invaluable. It was called "Delight Your Marriage- Christian Intimacy Transformation." He decided that this podcast would change our relationship. It would be a miracle cure. He was especially hopeful because it was a "Christian" podcast. He knew I was a very religious person and so appealing to my faith would be his ticket for even more control. And maybe, just maybe, it would elevate me to "Christian" status in his mind. While this podcast is a good one with good information, his aim was to use it against me for all the wrong reasons. He had absolutely no personal changes that he needed to make. He was certain that he was perfect. So this podcast, this relationship transformation, was just for me and the changes I needed to make. This podcast would surely cure me. It would be my transformation. I would learn how to prioritize my husband and make him feel that he is the king of his castle. My husband decided that a few days in the car could be turned into a teachable moment. He loved to teach, after all, and the car could be a fantastic, distraction free, classroom. Instead of listening to any music on this trip I would instead be learning how to delight my marriage.

On day two of our trip as we were making our way down the interstate, my husband dropped a small piece of paper on the floor of the car. It looked like trash, crumpled up with some handwritten notes jotted down. As he was driving he was expending great effort trying to reclaim this piece of paper. I couldn't figure out what was so important about it and when I questioned him he sharply responded, "I just need it, okay?" After fumbling around for a bit he finally grasped it between his fingers, and when he picked it up I captured a glance. It was a list of numbers. Numbers of podcast episodes. He had listened to and pre-planned exactly which episodes he wanted me to hear. This was literally a lesson plan, a curriculum of sorts, that he had created, and I was disheartened with his meticulous planning. This trip, this time in the car, wouldn't be about taking our firstborn to college. It would be nothing more than academics designed to teach me to be a better wife.

After two days of delightful podcast episodes I was feeling anything but delightful. I was feeling like an angry wife. I had listened to countless episodes, trying not to doze off in the middle of them. My patience was wearing thin and I was glad to arrive at my daughter's school and new home away from home. We spent the next few days getting her moved in to her new apartment and setting her up to begin her first year of college in a new state. There was a lot of work involved in getting her settled, as well as a lot of emotion that comes with dropping your first child off at college. My husband had been in my ear since before we left home, reminding me that he had planned this small side trip on for our return back to Texas. He had booked the hotel, made reservations, tickets and more, and he wouldn't stand for anything getting in his way or changing his itinerary. He reiterated this to me every single day. "If there are any delays with the move-in, or you decide you need an extra day, I am leaving you there and you can find your own way home." He was going on his mini vacation come hell or high water. There would be no schedule changes. The reservations were set in stone and he would not alter one minute of his vacation.

Knowing I had a limited amount of time to get my daughter settled, I worked non-stop, and by the end of our time there I had made some progress. I really needed an extra day, but there was no way I would broach this subject with my husband. However, there was just one sizable problem. The air conditioning in my daughter's apartment had quit working. It was July in Atlanta, Georgia, and the temperature inside her apartment the day before we departed was 93 degrees. I was in a panic. The apartment complex said they would need to order parts. It might be a few days before the problem could be resolved. And I had to leave or my husband was leaving without me. The next day I promised my daughter that I would continue to handle this problem from the road and we headed out of town, leaving our daughter to roast in a miserably hot apartment many miles from home.

I spent a good deal of our car trip that day on the phone. I was talking with the apartment maintenance department, trying to establish a timeline for the AC repair. I then spent time perusing the Target app, looking for the best fans to provide a temporary solution and then purchasing and arranging delivery to my daughter's apartment. My husband was annoyed, to say the least. He didn't want me to spend time on the phone. He wanted me to give him all my attention. Don't worry about the air conditioning, pay attention me! He wasn't the least bit concerned about the temperature in my daughter's apartment, or at least he didn't seem to be. He was on vacation, after all. Nothing was going to inconvenience him. I worried about rising room temperatures while he worried that I wasn't focusing on the podcast that was playing on the stereo. I was miserable but managing to put on a good show, acting like I was having a great time. It was vacation, after all. I had successfully managed to have fans delivered to my daughter. I hoped and prayed for cooler temperatures in Atlanta and decided I was going to give this vacation a chance.

We arrived at our destination the next day. We had decided to visit our college town in Tennessee for a few days and tour the campus, visiting all of our old stomping grounds. This is the place where we had met for the first time. The place where it had all began. I was excited. I hadn't visited my campus in many years and so much had changed. I couldn't wait to visit my old dorm buildings, the music building where I had spent so much time, and maybe even bump into a professor or two. We had reservations at a beautiful hotel right across from the campus and we planned to do a lot of walking and exploring. After checking into our room, we set out on foot. I had so many good memories of this place, and I felt so much nostalgia being back there again, walking around like I was a student. I was ready for a fun trip down memory lane. As we walked through this beautiful historic campus I noticed that we were passing up every single one of "my places." We walked right past my dorm buildings, right past the music school, right past anything that pertained to me and my college experience. I thought maybe we were going to see my husband's places first, then circle back and see mine, so I said nothing. After all, he had planned this trip and his plans were not to be messed with or altered. He was the master planner. We were going to see his dorms, his class buildings, his places, and we did just that. We toured around inside the buildings, even visiting classrooms and labs where he enjoyed some of his favorite engineering courses. While it was interesting, I was also confused and honestly I wanted to see where this was heading. When would it be time to do my tour? I was patient. My tour would be next, I was pretty sure. Then my husband said something that truly shocked me. "Well, I think we've seen everything we came to see. Are you ready to go to dinner?" I was speechless. I didn't even know what to say or think. My head was literally spinning. I was experiencing shock, anger, hurt, and a host of other emotions, and I simply said, "Sure, let's go eat." Was this guy serious? He was. He was finished with the campus tour.

At dinner I finally spoke up and asked why we hadn't toured any of the places that I had come to see. My husband acted genuinely surprised and so innocently he said, "Oh, did you want to see some things too?" It had never crossed his mind. I had been a student here, too. I had lived here for four years just as he had, and I had just as many memories of this place as he did. But it never once occurred to him that I might want to revisit my college experience. It was always just about him. The next day we returned to the campus and I got to visit the places I had come to see. It was an enjoyable experience, but my husband's callousness the previous day was still fresh on my mind. His self centeredness had literally blown me away. It became clear to me that day that life had come full circle. This place where our relationship had begun so many years ago, this college campus. This is where, in my heart, it was all going to end.

24

A Scratch on the Floor

Anyone who has experienced life with a narcissist will agree that these types of people don't handle stress well at all. High levels of stress can make them feel as though they are losing control. And a perceived loss of control can sometimes trigger narcissistic rage, or a narcissistic collapse. This is just what I witnessed near the end of my marriage when we were preparing to sell our home and downsize to a smaller house. Our children were growing up and one had already left the nest. Major life changes are stressful, and everyone knows that. But to my husband this change was almost unbearable. He had never handled stress well, but the level of stress involved in this particular upcoming move was clearly more than he could handle. His behavior became erratic and I was trying to spend less and less time with him. Any chance I got, I was distancing myself. He noticed, and he was angry. He was supposed to be the number one priority after all. Then it all came crashing down the day he discovered a scratch on the floor.

It seemed that the painters who were doing an interior paint job in our house had scooted a piece of furniture across the floor resulting in a small scratch in the wood. My husband had told me that morning before the painters arrived, that I need to warn them about this particular piece of furniture. And I did just that. When they began their work for the day, I showed them the piece in question and asked them to please not move it. Maybe they did, maybe they didn't. Maybe another one of the contractors saw a need to move that piece, as there were many people working in our home that day. Or maybe, just maybe, the scratch was already there. Who knows? It wasn't a catastrophe, but to my husband it was the end of the world. His rage toward me became frightening. In the driveway, and out of earshot of the painters, he proceeded to berate me like never before. "Why can't you follow instructions? Why are you so stupid? You mess up everything you do!" While he was hurling these words at me he was also clapping his hands together about an inch from my face. He wanted to make sure his intimidation tactics were in full force. This was the first time I had entertained the idea that he might actually hit me. He didn't, but I could see in his eyes that he wanted to so badly. He was so incredibly close to making this a physical altercation.

My husband proceeded to remind me that it was my job to watch the painters all day to make sure they didn't touch that single piece of furniture. "I was supposed to stand there and watch them for 8 hours?" I asked. "YES," he replied. I was baffled. He was serious. He thought that my simple warning to the painters had not been enough. He really thought I should have stood guard for the entire day to avoid having the floor accidentally scratched. This made sense to him. Complete, perfect sense. And then he followed up this ridiculous claim with the words, "Get out of here and don't ever come back!" But note that there were some expletives thrown in there for good measure. He was kicking me out because of a scratch on the floor? He actually wasn't joking. He then proceeded to tell me that he would change the settings on the security system so that I wouldn't be able to enter the house again. At that point I was pretty sure I never wanted to enter that house again. I gladly left. In fact I couldn't wait to leave. And I never wanted to return. But I did.

An hour later he called, confused as to where I was and why I had left him to handle the house prep all by himself. I had driven to my parents house and I was planning to spend the remainder of the day there in peace. "Come back, I need you here," he bellowed into the phone. I was so confused. "But you told me to leave and never come back," I said. He had no response. Neither did I. I knew there was work to be done at home, and I was motivated to get our house sold, so back I went. I had just witnessed a terribly sinister side to my husband, and the wheels were turning in my head. I wasn't sure how much longer I could endure this lifestyle.

MIND BOGGLING BEHAVIORS OF A NARCISSIST

They walk ahead of you.

My husband walked ahead of me 100% of the time. I found this so odd, and I questioned him about it often. His response was always the same. "You walk too slow. I can't walk that slow." The real reason narcissists tend to walk in front is to exert their authority. They are the master and you are the servant. Walking in front of you creates a visual representation of that dynamic.

They get angry when you're injured or sick.

Being injured or sick was beyond miserable in my house. A sick or injured person cannot be of any use to a narcissist. When sick, I could not provide supply for my husband. I wasn't at his beck and call to praise him and serve him. An ill partner is nothing but an inconvenience for a narcissist.

They traumatize you before important events or holidays.

My husband's behavior often deteriorated around the holidays. Just the same, he would seem to find reasons to be mad at me before we attended important events. We went to many events not speaking or with him pouting miserably. Important events ultimately steal the spotlight from the narcissist and this creates a bad attitude. In their world, nothing should steal their spotlight.

They don't answer questions directly.

Direct answers didn't exist in our house. A simple question could yield a one hour answer. My husband had to explain and over explain and explain again. No short answers. Nothing in our life was simple. Complicated was the norm. Narcissists have to be right all of the time, and over explaining and drawing out answers make them look knowledgable.

Their gift giving always has strings attached.

My husband loved to give me gifts. He took great pride in it. But every gift had a motive behind it. Sometimes he gave me gifts in front of my parents or others just so he could prove to everyone what a great person he was, how thoughtful, how caring. This was an angle he loved to use. He would then remind me daily about what he had given me. It became exhausting and it was honestly easier to not receive gifts from him. If a narcissist wants to give you a gift, you probably don't want it once you understand the implications behind the gift giving.

They are jealous of children and pets.

Any time spent dealing with kids or pets was notated by my husband. He wanted to make sure I spent equal or more time with him. His jealousy was out of control at all times. Children and pets take time and care, and there is no room in a narcissist's world for anyone to receive care but them.

They use sleep deprivation as a means to control you.

I was more or less sleep deprived for most of my marriage. In the later years my husband would go as far as to be angry at me if I fell asleep before him. He did not like it when I slept and saw it as a sign of weakness. Sleep deprivation also keeps a person in an over-tired, fog like state, making them easier to control and manipulate.

They assume everyone is jealous of them.

My husband was absolutely convinced that everyone wanted everything he had. He was so sure everyone was jealous of him. This led to fairly severe paranoia. As the years went on he became more and more security conscious. While this isn't necessarily a bad thing, he took it to the extreme, as he did with most things. Multiple security cameras and alarms, fire-arms, extra locks on doors, financial and identity theft precautions, nothing evaded my husband. He stayed on guard all the time.

They are easily bored.
If my husband wasn't being praised and doted on, then he was bored. He liked adventure at all turns and simple activities at home were ridiculous to him. He wanted to be entertained in grand fashion. Narcissists can't ever be satisfied enough, entertained enough, or happy enough. They need more and more and more to combat their ever growing boredom.

They diminish your accomplishments.
Any accomplishments I achieved were always downplayed. They were seen as cute yet insignificant. His accomplishments were to be celebrated by everyone in the family, no matter how small. Narcissists have to be the best at everything and will create competition even with their kids or their spouse. In their mind, no one should accomplish more or be celebrated more than the narcissist.

25

Marriage Counseling

In the 28th year of our marriage, after our oldest child had left the nest for college, my husband decided that we needed to go to counseling. This sounded like a great idea. I was miserable. He was miserable. Counseling was going to fix it all. He researched, as he did so well, and found a therapist that he thought could fix our marriage, or more accurately, fix me. Our intake session was a good one. We answered a bunch of questions and put some of our concerns on the table. His largest concern centered around intimacy, or lack thereof. Something was surely wrong with me. We just couldn't form a connection and it was most definitely due to my faults. He wanted the therapist to fix me. It should be a simple fix. She should just reiterate how great he is. Smart, wealthy, driven. Who wouldn't want to be married to him?

The next few sessions with the therapist involved a lot more question/answer events. She was trying to establish exactly what our dynamic was. She asked a question one day that was a "deal sealer" for her, although I didn't realize it at the time. The question was this: "Tell me about your bucket list." My husband went first. And he went on, and on and on. Places he wanted to travel to, things he wanted to accomplish, all of the fun he wanted to have. Fun, fun and more fun, and on and on and on and on. Finally it was my turn. "Tell me about your bucket list, " the therapist said. A long silent pause. My husband is looking at me with disgust on his face. The silence continues. And then I finally speak. "I don't think I have one." The therapist tries to help me along. "What are your goals? Where would you like to travel? What are your dreams?" All I could say was, "I don't know. I don't think I have any." For the life of me I couldn't think of ONE THING to say. She looked at me for a bit. She didn't seem confused. She seemed like she had just validated what she had been suspecting, but I was still in the dark.

After a few more joint sessions with the marriage therapist she was beginning to get a good read on our dynamic and our situation. She was figuring us out as a couple. During one particular session my husband was prattling on about my issues. "She prioritizes the kids over me. She loves the kids more than me. She ignores me," and so on down the line. As was the norm, I sat on the sofa next to him, quietly listening and taking it all in. I enjoyed studying the facial expressions of the therapist as my husband would venture on his tirades about all my faults. As he was muttering endlessly the therapist finally stopped him. She asked him a very direct question, and it shocked me just a bit. "You come in here every week and spend the entire session discussing everything you don't like about your wife. If you are so miserable, why don't you just leave this marriage?" There was a long uncomfortable pause. Then he spoke. "I can't. That would make me the bad guy. My family would be mad at me and so would her family. I don't want to look like the bad guy." One might think that his response would be something more along the lines of, "I can't because I love her." But this was not his reasoning at all. He was only concerned with how a failed marriage would make him look. His image- this was the only thing that mattered to him. This marriage had been a lie, and I began asking myself if he had ever actually loved me. I was pretty sure I knew the answer sitting there in the therapist's office, and today I am sure I know the answer. He did not love me. He had never loved me. He loved the idea of me. He loved how I could make him look and how I could serve him. But he did not and had not ever loved me. He had only been interested in protecting and promoting his false image that he was selling to the world.

I had been looking forward to the one-on-one meeting with the therapist that was upcoming. After our joint sessions together she wanted to do individual meetings with us. This sounded interesting. I decided that maybe I should ask her about the topics I had been reading about on the internet. Toxic relationships, emotional abuse and covert narcissism. After the life altering instagram post I had read about intimacy, I had been educating myself on these things after all, and I was pretty well versed on these topics. I didn't waste any time in our therapy session. After sitting down on the therapist's sofa I bravely said, "Um, I think I'm being abused." I couldn't believe I was even uttering those words. It seemed so accusatory, and what if I was wrong? What horrible things would she think about me? It was a tense moment, and her reply shook me. "You are." And my world finally made sense. 27 years of questions, doubts, fear, insecurity. She had noticed my constant apologizing and my willingness to take the blame for all the problems in my marriage. She saw a clear example of coercive control when speaking with me. She had watched me week after week sit silently while my husband rambled on and on about everything that was wrong with me. She saw that I made no effort to defend myself. She had been studying our dynamics and she had gotten an accurate read. She was clearly concerned about my well being. She asked if she could email me some information. She told me she would send it discreetly, with a bogus subject line, so that in case my husband snooped into my e-mail it would not look suspicious. I had never even considered that he might pry into my emails, but the plan sounded smart. I told her I would gladly accept any information she could send.

Later that evening I opened my inbox to find that the therapist had sent three website links. The email subject read "Intimacy" and she had titled the links "Intimacy in Marriage," "Building Strong Relationships" and "Marriage Issues." It looked as though she was sending me links that pertained to our therapy sessions. My husband would suspect nothing if in fact he prodded into my e-mails. As I clicked each of these links my head began to spin. I couldn't believe what I was reading. This therapist was concerned and these web links proved it: An article on emotional abuse. A website with information on domestic violence. And lastly, a link to my local women's shelter.

"The only thing more unthinkable than leaving was staying; the only thing more impossible than staying was leaving. I didn't want to destroy anything or anybody. I just wanted to slip quietly out the back door, without causing any fuss or consequences, and then not stop running until I reached Greenland."

— Elizabeth Gilbert
Eat, Pray, Love

26

Leaving

After my encounter with the therapist I was feeling more validated, and I knew I needed to get out. Fast. When reading about covert narcissism on the internet I came across a phrase that stuck with me. "Run. Don't walk." And so I crafted a plan. I knew I couldn't just leave or tell him I was leaving. It seemed too risky. I had to be more gradual. So I began to spend more time at my parent's house, making up reasons why I needed to be there. And then I began spending the night there a few nights a week. "My mom isn't feeling well, so I'm going to stay with her tonight. I'll be back in the morning." And so on. And then one day I just didn't come back. I got up the courage to tell him I needed some time and some space. I was struggling. I was going to stay with my parents for a while. He scoffed. He couldn't imagine why I needed time. He provided a perfect life for me. My "weakness" was disgusting him. Meanwhile, I was sleeping. I slept for days. My body was completely spent. I had never felt more tired in my entire life. It was physical exhaustion combined with mental exhaustion. My energy level was at a zero. It was clear that if I had waited any longer to get out I might have experienced a major health event. I had escaped in the nick of time.

During this time I located a therapist who had some experience with treating victims of narcissistic abuse. I looked forward to our first session because this would be an opportunity for me to gain a second opinion. I was still feeling the need to be validated in my assumption that I was an abuse victim. In some way, it still felt like a bold title and it felt so accusatory. Abuser and victim. Those were words not to be used flippantly. At our first intake session I gave the therapist a fairly thorough rundown of what I had experienced in my 28 years of marriage to a narcissist. I wanted to be accurate and clear in all of my depictions. During this session I found that explaining my experiences to another person made me realize just how damaging the abuse in my marriage had been. As I found myself relaying these stories I almost couldn't believe it. These stories sounded so much worse when I spoke them rather than just let them occupy space in my head. Why had I endured this for so long? I felt confused, guilty, angry and mentally exhausted. By the end of our first session, the therapist had completely validated my feelings. Before I left her office I asked a question that had been on my mind for the entirety of the session. "Based on your experience, exactly how bad was my abuse?" Her reply was, "One of the worst, if not the worst I've ever dealt with."

After a few sessions with my new therapist, I began to realize that reconciling with my husband would be a recipe for disaster. She advised me that if I were to return he would consider that a win in his playbook. And while things might be good for a while, statistics show that the abuse would eventually return and only be worse. This made sense to me, and I couldn't take that chance. I had successfully made a break, and retreating back wasn't going to be in my future plans. I began returning to our home during the days when he was at work to retrieve personal items and clothes. Just a few at a time so as not to be obvious that I was actually moving out. I made frequent visits to the ATM to draw out a little cash each time. Again, nothing too obvious. When I went to the grocery story I would request cash back, building up some funds little by little. I retrieved important documents and immediately began making a list of all of our bank accounts and information that would be necessary for a divorce filing.

Days turned to weeks and his anger grew, and so did my fear. He wanted to meet and talk. Surely we could work this out. All I needed to do was make a few changes, or so he said. If I could change a few things then he would be happy and we could live happily ever after. This would be an easy fix. Why was I making it so complicated? I met him at a coffee shop. It was uncomfortable. He gave me all the reasons that I should return. I should stop this silly charade. We needed to get on with our life. We had big plans, and his plans were not going to be altered. He promised he would be better. He said he would be nicer, provided I could make changes too. Just make him my number one priority. It was so simple in his mind. I found it incredibly difficult to be direct with him. I would instead promise to think about it, but deep inside I had already made my decision.

"There's a phrase, "the elephant in the living room", which purports to describe what it's like to live with a drug addict, an alcoholic, an abuser. People outside such relationships will sometimes ask, 'How could you let such a business go on for so many years? Didn't you see the elephant in the living room?' And it's so hard for anyone living in a more normal situation to understand the answer that comes closest to the truth; 'I'm sorry, but it was there when I moved in. I didn't know it was an elephant; I thought it was part of the furniture.' There comes an a-ha moment for some folks - the lucky ones - when they suddenly recognize the difference."

— Stephen King

27

A Meeting

A couple of months after my departure, my husband decided it was time to pull out all the stops. I hadn't returned to him and he needed to do something about it. His plan of action was to meet with my parents. Sounds perplexing, but it gets even stranger. For this meeting my husband drove 500 miles to catch my parents while they were spending a few weeks at their second home in another state. He decided this would be the best scenario. I wouldn't know about this meeting, and he could have their undivided attention without me around. My husband showed up at my parents' home unannounced. Their telephone rang, and it was him. "I'm here, outside your house." I can only imagine the shock on their faces. Such an impromptu gesture was very atypical of him.

My husband made his way into my parents' home with an

armful of notebooks, three ring binders and all of his necessary materials. He was going to give them an actual presentation. But not just any presentation. This was an entire pre-planned speech about everything that was wrong with their daughter. All the things that I needed to change in order for him to be happy. Was this damage control or complete sociopathic behavior? Who knows, but it was definitely bizarre by all standards. My parents took a seat at the kitchen table, curious what he was going to say. He began by giving my parents an explicit speech about the childhood trauma that he had endured. He explained to them that as a result of this trauma he required excessive attention and affection, even more than the average person. After all, he is special and nothing is ever really enough in his world. I was failing on every front, but he was sure I could make some improvements. Confused and baffled, my parents listened politely for a ridiculous amount of time, and then attempted to explain that I needed some space, that he was suffocating me and that his controlling behavior was raising red flags for them all over the place. He denied being controlling. He was just a very attentive husband, and that was a good thing in his mind. They should be proud they had a son-in-law like him.

The meeting progressed on for several exhausting hours. My husband was utterly convinced that if he talked long enough he would gain my parents' support and they could assist him in talking some sense into me. Either that, or he thought he could just wear them down, as he had done to me on many occasions. He felt that my parents were his best bet for success- the people whose opinions I valued the most. He just needed to make his case to them and he would be home free. They would most definitely agree with his list of improvements that I needed to make and we could just wrap this chapter up and get on with our life of luxury. Only it didn't happen that way. He had hit an impasse with my parents. They didn't give him an inch, and he was astounded and probably fuming angry beneath the surface. He ultimately packed up his binders and notebooks, got in his car and drove 500 miles home. His plan had failed. It was back to the drawing board.

The question that loomed after this bizarre confrontation with my parents was this: Did he actually want me back or was he merely doing damage control? Recalling his comment to our therapist about not being able to leave the marriage due to a possible hit to his character, I had to wonder what his motive really was when he drove 1,000 miles round trip for this meeting. His behavior had been growing more and more erratic over the past year and he was growing meaner, angrier and hostile with each passing day. It was possible, I thought, that he was trying to force me out. To make life so impossibly miserable that I would just leave on my own. Perhaps this was his master plan to dissolve the marriage without being "the bad guy." While it seems like this was his agenda, and it probably was, he was also likely conflicted. He didn't really want to be alone. It wasn't suiting his lifestyle or his image. He didn't love me and didn't necessarily want to remain in a marriage with me, but his ego was telling him differently.

After retuning home from his failed trip, nothing changed. I continued to live independently and we continued to converse by phone on occasion. After finding out about his trip to see my parents, I was both confused and angry. The fact that he would put them in such an uncomfortable position infuriated me. And the bizarreness of his behavior concerned me. During a conversation shortly after his return, I questioned him about his intentions. He responded by defending his actions. He stated that he had driven 1,000 miles to speak to my parents in an effort to get me back. The funny thing was this- he never spoke to my parents about how to "get me back." His hours-long speech only detailed what he didn't like about me. Was he lying to me or was he delusional? Who knows? But this stunt did nothing to help matters. In fact, it raised even more red flags.

28

Coffee and Calls

As my life of newfound peace moved onward, there were more invites to coffee, more texts, and more phone calls. His plan with my parents had failed, so my husband had now decided that constant contact would be his best bet to convince me to return and restore our family. During one phone call he stated, "You need to come back. This isn't working for me." A statement only a narcissist could make. It wasn't working for him. But was it working for me? In his mind that didn't matter. In his mind nothing mattered but him, the covert narcissist. The longer I stayed away the bolder I got, and during one phone conversation I finally worked up the nerve to ask him a question that had perplexed me for years. "Do you remember the blackmail incident?" I asked. He stammered and then paused. There was a long, uncomfortable silence. No, he really didn't remember. He wasn't completely sure what I was talking about.

I continued. "The blackmail, the loaded gun, do you recall this?" He replied, "Well, now that you mention it I vaguely remember something, I think. I'm not sure." It was clear to me that he really wasn't sure. He had traumatized me and he actually didn't remember it. It occupied no space in his brain. He really didn't remember this incident. The confusion in his voice and his blank reply were genuine. "Well, whatever it was, I guess I'm sorry for it, " he said. He guessed he was sorry for something he didn't even remember. I didn't exactly consider that a genuine apology. I was shocked, but I let it go. There was no sense in hashing through something that clearly had made no impression on him whatsoever. He didn't recall this traumatic event. This event literally changed the way my brain processed trauma. This event left internal scars inside of me that will never ever go away. It left me with flashbacks that I'll relive for the rest of my life. But to my narcissistic husband it had just been another Tuesday.

Eventually I started turning my husband's invites down. I could not see a resolution to this marriage in any way, shape or form. No amount of coffee dates would change this stark reality. There was simply no path forward. We had continued with our marriage counseling, seeing the therapist once a week even though we were living apart by this point. I was still seeking validation and I found our sessions interesting. As was the norm, my husband did the majority of the talking during these sessions. I continued to sit quietly and laugh to myself as I watched the ever changing facial expressions of our therapist as she tried to grasp the absurdity of my husband's mindset. After each session was over, my husband and I would depart without saying a word to each other. We would get into our separate cars and return to our separate homes. This system of separate lives was working for me.

Our final meeting with the marriage therapist was quite interesting. When we arrived, we didn't know it would be our last meeting, but by the end of the session the therapist had decided she would not be seeing us again. She actually went so far as to kick my husband out of therapy. I didn't think it was possible to get kicked out of therapy, but I watched it happen before my very own two eyes. At the end of our session this woman looked at my husband and stated, "I can't help you anymore. You are not able to see things from other people's perspectives and therefore there is nothing more I can do for you." She went on to say that while she would love to continue taking our money, she simply could not ethically do so. She had hit a brick wall with my husband. He was clearly above her pay grade. In fact, he was probably above anyone's pay grade. He was not self aware, she had just confirmed, and that was never going to change. She clearly saw no path for us, and I was perfectly okay with that. She was very professional in her assessment and wished us well. She genuinely hoped that we would both find happiness. Perhaps most importantly though, she had once again added to my validation that I so desperately needed.

I lessened my contact with my husband and only texted when we needed to discuss the kids. I was seeing less and less of him, slowly making a break. It felt safer this way as opposed to a sudden split. I had read that it was recommended to go "no contact" when leaving a relationship with a narcissist. No communication whatsoever to the point of blocking numbers. This didn't feel doable to me and I resisted this advice. I felt that "no contact" would further my husband's anger and I had no motivation to do that.   Instead, I opted for a slowing down in communication. Weeks turned to months, and it was clear that I wasn't coming back. The slowing eventually came to a halt. It was over. 29 years of marriage had come to a close, and not any too soon.

TIPS FOR LEAVING A NARCISSIST

Keep your plans confidential
If your narcissistic partner learns that you are planning to leave, things could potentially become dangerous. Narcissists don't react well to rejection and they will thwart any plans they become privy to. The safest way out is a quiet departure.

Document everything, take photos and screenshots
Taking photographs of bank statements, account numbers and anything else pertinent is very important. Don't delete any text messages and screen shot anything that could be of use in illustrating dynamics and character.

Gather your important documents (Social Security card, birth certificate, passport)
While you will most certainly get these documents eventually, it is much easier to take them with you when you leave your partner, provided you have access to them. It saves a hassle down the road if you keep these things in your possession.

Keep a supply of cash on hand
Cash is important in an emergency, and it is always a good idea to keep some cash on hand. Drawing small amounts at a time out of the ATM is a good idea, as well as requesting cash back when you make purchases at stores.

Set up a support system of people that you trust
If you are planning to leave it is important to let someone know what you are doing. Make arrangements for where you will stay and bring friends and family into your loop to provide emotional support.

Locate a therapist in your area

Therapists can do wonders, especially when you are dealing with a flood of emotions after leaving an abusive partner. A therapist can help to validate your feelings as well.

Don't give your abuser "one more chance"

Inevitably your partner will want another chance. Narcissists will promise you the moon, just to save their ego. Statistics show that when you return to an abusive spouse the abuse ultimately gets worse. This is because they have won you back and they know they'll win you back again and again. Once you make the decision to leave an abuser, do not return.

29

C-PTSD and Healing

Healing from narcissistic abuse is a complicated matter. I was dealing with a multitude of emotions, primarily guilt. I felt horrible. I had upended my husband's life. I had broken our family apart. I woke up each morning feeling well rested and re-lieved...and guilty. "I ruined his life," I said over and over to my therapist. She replied, "No, he ruined his life." It took months for that statement to sink into my head and actually stick. With much needed rest came more clarity, and over time the guilt began to lessen. The fog began to lift. I came to understand that my guilt was a symptom of something called Complex Post Traumatic Stress Disorder, C-PTSD, and this was a turning point in my healing journey.

I had heard of Post Traumatic Stress Disorder and only

associated this with soldiers who had experienced war. My situation couldn't compare to this. What I didn't realize was that I had experienced a different form of war in my own home for years and years, and while PTSD and C-PTSD are different conditions, they share some similarities. Both conditions result from trauma, but slightly different types of trauma. Victims of PTSD have been traumatized by a single event or group of events and experience symptoms as a result. Victims of C-PTSD have been traumatized over a long period of time. Their trauma isn't sudden, it is steady. Trauma becomes a way of life for these victims, and they reach a state where they don't even recognize it as trauma anymore. Trauma is just their normal, and many victims don't have a clear point of reference for what "normal" looks like. This is exactly where I found myself.

So what does C-PTSD look like? For starters, most victims become hyper-vigilant. They are always waiting for the next problem, the next crisis, the other shoe to drop. Watching and waiting. I found after leaving my husband that I no longer trusted people. Aside from my immediate family and close friends, I assumed every person had an agenda. It almost created a paranoia for me. I found myself needing to build trust again with nearly every person I knew. Victims of C-PTSD also experience a great deal of guilt as I did, and some victims even experience some memory loss. Some people experience sleep disruption and recurring nightmares or flashbacks. My body was too exhausted for sleep disruptions, but looming memories and flashbacks don't fade easily.

Another symptom of C-PTSD is emotional numbness, and this was something I most definitely experienced in my healing journey. After the initial guilt began to subside, the numbness overtook me. I literally felt nothing for my narcissistic spouse. I felt no sadness and no nostalgia whatsoever. It was as if there was a light switch that had just been turned off. This numbness actually served to protect me, I believe, from overwhelming feelings. I had just learned that I was an abusive victim and had just walked out on a 29 year marriage. This was a lot to process, and my system just decided to feel numb. This numbness gave me time to work through my feelings and it felt strange but somewhat healthy at the same time.

Since C-PTSD is so complex indeed, it is quite difficult to recover from. The trauma has been ingrained in the victim for such a long time, and it is not easy to reverse. Healing can take a long time, and no two victims are on the same timeline. A lot of survivors of narcissistic abuse might feel a sense of mourning. Not mourning a death, but mourning a relationship that never really existed. A love that was never there. My marriage had basically been a lie and this was a hard pill to swallow. A 29 year lie is not something one recovers from overnight. A trauma informed therapist can be an immense help in processing these types of feelings, as well as good self care and a support system. Finally, a lot of patience with yourself is a must. Complex trauma requires complex healing.

Besides guilt, the other emotion I struggled with after leaving my narcissistic husband was anger. Not anger toward him, but anger toward myself. Why had I stayed in this marriage for so long? Why hadn't I seen the signs earlier? Why did I waste so many years being abused? I was furious. I felt like I had wasted a very large chunk of my life that I wouldn't get back again. How could I have been so stupid? I hadn't been happy in my marriage. There were happy times, yes, but I hadn't experienced a life of happiness and contentedness. Why did I stay? The answer is a complicated one and the reasons are many. I had been trauma bonded, for starters. Just walking away from a trauma bond is not exactly easy. I was dependent on him financially, and I had a comfortable life. I didn't want to share custody of my children while they were young. I could not fathom sharing them on holidays and such. That's not the kind of family life I wished to have.

Perhaps the biggest reason I stayed in this marriage for nearly 29 years was the simple fact that I had created a normal for myself. I didn't focus on the abuse. Instead it just became a way of life to which I adapted. It was my normal. It's what I knew. And leaving would upend it all. I had no idea where I would even begin. A new life was frightening to me. I had been convinced that I could never make it on my own. I wasn't capable. I didn't have the skill set, the financial sense, or the knowledge to live an independent life. This was the trauma bond speaking. I slowly began to learn that I had to forgive myself and I had to find my autonomy and rebuild my confidence. I had to heal and I had to move on. I was lucky to have made my exit successfully and it was time for me to start living my life now, not his.

Aside from the help of a good therapist, I found a lot of answers through a podcast, "The Covert Narcissism Podcast." Renee Swanson is the host of this program, and she too was a victim of a covert narcissistic spouse. Her stories were my stories, and I found so much validation listening to her speak. This program also taught me how to begin to heal and how to adjust my mindset. As I listened to Renee discuss her healing, my own guilt continued to abate and my confidence in myself began to grow. I read a lot of self help books on narcissism and related topics, and found these resources to be as helpful as the weekly therapy that I was attending.

Ultimately the best healer for me was simply talking. Talking about what I had experienced. Talking about the trauma. It was freeing to tell my story. I had held my trauma inside for so long and it was finally time to release it. When I began telling my story I was surprised to find so many other women and men who had been or are currently in similar situations.

I found that narcissistic abuse is much more widespread than I ever imagined. I discovered so many who were searching for answers, validation and help, just as I had been. The more we learn to talk and acknowledge this form of abuse, the more we can heal and save others from these dire circumstances.

30

The Monetary Value of Domestic Abuse

A year after I left my narcissistic husband I gathered the courage to file for divorce. A year is a long time, but confidence builds slowly. When I was finally ready I called a divorce attorney and put the wheels in motion. I was getting ready to turn 50, and it seemed like an appropriate time for a new beginning. As the petitioner of the divorce I cited "irreconcilable differences." This seemed fair. I had no intention of airing any dirty laundry. I assumed that my husband and I could come to an amicable agreement and things could run smoothly. I had my head in the clouds and momentarily forgot exactly who I was dealing with. In the blink of an eye my husband retained a high powered attorney and it was obvious he was ready to fight. His tone changed literally overnight. He went from begging me to return to him to putting all of his efforts into making my life miserable. His attitude went from one extreme to the other in a split second. From "love" to sheer hate in the snap of a finger. He responded to the petition with a counter-petition, citing that I was guilty of "cruelty" toward him. I'm still not sure how he reasoned this accusation. I suppose I was cruel for leaving a cruel environment. It made no sense to me, and it caught me completely off guard. He made it clear he was going to play hard ball. This divorce would be no walk in the park.

My narcissistic husband was angry. In fact, he was irate. These divorce papers were the ultimate betrayal. No one leaves or betrays a narcissist. It simply isn't an acceptable move. But when it does happen, life becomes difficult for all of those involved. My husband's first maneuver was to file a petition to take possession of my car. He stated that he owned all of our vehicles and that I should not be allowed to enter or operate my own car. This was a completely absurd move, and needless to say, this motion was struck down. It did, however, set the tone for what was to come. Like a spoiled child, everything we owned suddenly belonged to him. His money, his vehicles, his possessions. In his mind, I owned nothing. It was clear that I would have to fight for every penny, nickel and dime that was rightfully mine.

The next maneuvers involved wild spending sprees. My husband began liquidating trust accounts that he had held for our entire marriage but had never once touched. God forbid that I should benefit in any way from "his" separate property money. The same week that he petitioned to take my car from me, he used a portion of his separate funds to purchase a luxury beach home. He was letting me see just what I had walked away from. His attempt was to make me jealous, while impressing his children with his vast wealth. The toys soon followed. A speed boat, jet skis, golf carts, and on and on. If he was going to be single he was going to do it in style. This level of spending was completely out of character for my husband. We had always lived comfortably, but somewhat frugal as well. He was making a point with his beach house and his toys. He was showing me just how big his trust fund was and just how much money I could have had if only I had stayed and endured more abuse. No thank you.

It wasn't just the trust fund that was taking a hit. It was also our joint bank account. If he travelled, he only flew first class. If he stayed in a hotel he got a suite. If he went to dinner he made sure to get appetizers, drinks and dessert. A typical dinner bill would run him about $200.00. No worries, though. He had plenty of money. I simply couldn't keep up with his spending, try as I might. He outspent me 10 fold and kept our "community" fund as low as possible. He was doing nothing illegal, technically, but pushing the limits as far as he could. He was living the high life and his narcissism was becoming more overt. He had just suffered the ultimate betrayal, and he had to save face. He had to remind everyone, including himself, just how important he was.

I hired a legal team to work on account tracing, and my team did a thorough job. However, we were a bit dismayed at what we found. At the end of the day my husband had the best people in charge of his money and had been protecting his funds for years. Probably all the way back to the beginning of our marriage. He had accounts fixed that I couldn't touch. He had seemingly been covering himself in the event of divorce for 29 years. Deep inside, perhaps he knew he was an abuser. Perhaps he knew someday I would cease to accept his abuse. Or maybe not. It might have just been that narcissistic, self absorbed attitude. It all belonged to him and no one else. In his mind, he who dies with the most toys wins.

Our divorce was in the working stage for about 8 months. It was a stressful 8 months with lots of meetings and planning and calculating. My husband was a wealthy man. I had been married to him for 29 years. I had given birth to his two children. And I had endured years of his mistreatment. It stood to reason that I would walk away from this nightmare marriage with enough money to live on comfortably for the rest of my life. I never gave it a second thought. I live in a 50/50 state, so by law I would be assured to get my 50 percent. The problem was this. Our "community" fund was a mere fraction of his "separate property" fund. It was a bit disheartening. However, with some figuring it seemed that I could likely be awarded a disproportionate amount of our community property. After all, this man was an abuser, and I had people lined up to testify in my favor. A 60/40 percent split seemed doable. I could live with that. It certainly wouldn't be fair, but it would be a decent amount of funds, and I could leave this marriage far behind me.

The day of divorce mediation arrived 9 months after my initial filing. This was it. I was confident that I would emerge from that room happy and free. My lawyer and I set up shop in the conference room at her office. My husband was at his lawyer's office in a different building, and our mediator was on a Zoom call. It seemed like a good system, especially good because I wouldn't have to be face to face with my abuser. We spent the day exchanging offers and counteroffers back and forth. It seemed that my life had been reduced to a giant math equation and I was solving for "ex." One hour into our 10 hour ordeal it was obvious that things were not going to end as expected. My husband was only willing to give up 50 percent. Just what he had to give by law. I was appalled and insulted, and he didn't appear to be negotiable in the least. The day wore on and I wore down. My team discussed what my options were and what amount I could expect a judge to award me, should we decide to take our case to court. However, going to court would mean more legal fees and further draining of the community funds. It was a tough call, but in the end it was decided that court was too risky. There wouldn't be enough gain in that route for me. I was ready for closure and so I decided to settle.

After more arguing and counter-offering the final number landed at 51.95% in my favor. After 10 hours of negotiating, my husband had agreed to this, begrudgingly. I asked our mediator before I consented to this offer and signed on the dotted line, "What about the abuse? Where does that factor in?" There was a brief silence. Then he spoke. His answer left me somewhat stunned and speechless. "Well, that's accounted for in the disproportionate split," he said. So if I do the math correctly, domestic abuse is worth 1.95%. 29 years of emotional abuse, and it only cost my husband 1.95%. I was supposed to be happy that I got more than half of the community share. My husband felt he had been generous. In truth, he had awarded me a mere 10% of his net worth. He would be laughing all the way to the bank. My portion of the settlement mainly consisted of retirement accounts that I couldn't access for several more years without paying huge penalties, in addition to stock accounts that would ultimately take a couple of months to transfer into my name. I would be leaving my lawyer's office that evening with only the money in my purse- a five dollar bill.

My husband was proud of his money, and he wasn't about to give up a penny more than he needed to. After all, it had been my choice to leave him. Therefore, in his mind, I deserved nothing. I had walked away from him, and therefore I had walked away from "his" money. He was forgetting, however, that we built a good deal of our wealth together. We had been a good team and we had made smart financial decisions. Newly married and fresh out of college, we spent our one year wedding anniversary at Taco Bell. This became somewhat of a joke through the years and a very popular and endearing story to tell our friends and family. We made a habit of it. Every year on our wedding anniversary we ate dinner at Taco Bell, from the days of frugal living to the days of vast wealth. It was funny, and it was tradition. However, thoughts of humor or tradition weren't on my mind when I left the divorce mediation that evening.

Freedom was all I could focus on. After 10 long hours I emerged from my lawyer's conference room free, though my happiness level was debatable. The monetary value of domestic abuse had proved to be sickening.

It was 7:00PM when the mediation ended. It had been a long and exhausting day for everyone. My ex husband would now likely head to his beach house for some much needed rest and relaxation, or perhaps he would simply retreat to his penthouse apartment. Whichever location he chose, he would probably be stopping for a lavish, expensive meal along the way. I headed out of the city, too, feeling tired and relieved, yet frustrated all at the same time. I was looking forward to going home to my comfortable and cozy townhome in the suburbs where I could enjoy a quiet evening knowing with confidence that the battle had been fought and I had emerged still standing. It wasn't about the money. It was about getting back my self respect, my value as a human being and my self esteem. You cannot put a price on that. On the way home I made a quick diversion to get a bite to eat. I decided to stop at Taco Bell. I did it for myself. Taco Bell would no longer be associated with traditions of a relationship that was over. It would now be associated with the beginning of my new life. That quick diversion to pick up my dinner at the drive thru was the first step on my new journey.

Epilogue

At the age of 19 I fell for a narcissist. Today I am learning to live again. My life is peaceful, quiet and simple. Occasionally it gets a little lonely, but when it does I stop and remind myself where I've come from. I never want to return to that level of chaos again. I like where I am now. My divorce is final and the hard fought battle is over. In the end I guess I can say I won- not because of any fair financial settlement, but because I got out. I survived. I'm alive and thriving, and that is a win for me.

One aspect that surprised me when I left my husband was how few friends stood by me. It was a bit painful to see how many people dropped out of sight. Some people probably didn't agree with my decision to leave. And most assuredly, some didn't want to bother themselves with the mess that I was stepping into. A divorce was looming after all, and I would need emotional support. Most people just checked out. It was easier that way. It is definitely true that when you go through a crisis, you find out who your real friends are. And I was finding out.

Shortly after leaving my marriage I ran across a quote and it spoke to me. It simply said, "Pay attention to who checks on you when you get a little quiet. Those are your people." I have a lot fewer people today than I had a few years ago, and I'm okay with that because mine are truly the best people.

My parents: They assisted me in escaping my abusive marriage, and without them I would most definitely still be living in a nightmare. They helped me financially until I could get on my feet. They made sure I felt safe and protected, always. They attended every legal meeting with me and showed support like I couldn't have imagined. I'm a survivor, not a statistic, and this is all thanks to them.

My kids: These two young people have shown me unwavering support. Even though I stayed in my marriage longer than I should have, my son and daughter still have my back. They work hard to maintain a relationship with their father. He is their father, after all. But they also make sure I know they are in my corner. I am proud of their integrity and their character. I go to sleep at night resting assured that I have placed two good people with good hearts on this Earth.

My best friend: My rock. My closest confidant. The one who has patiently listened to countless hours of my stories, counseling me and helping me stay level headed even when my emotions were all over the map. The one who messages me every morning without fail, making sure I have the confidence I need to embrace the day ahead. "I'll be here if you need me, love. You're the bravest girl I know."

These five. These are my people, and I am blessed.

Narcissism is touching far too many people in our society to-day. This abuse is so often hidden and many victims are unsure just how to acquire support. Lawyers, judges and all those involved in the divorce process oftentimes don't have a great deal of understanding about Narcissistic Personality Disorder and the cruel, vindictive and manipulating nature of these types of individuals. Knowledge is power, and narcissism needs to be called out for the damaging consequences it has on its victims. This white collar crime of domestic violence needs to be recognized for what it is. I hope by telling my story I can inspire those in need to reach out and seek the help they require and deserve. No one needs to suffer in silence. No one needs to suffer alone. Narcissistic abuse is all too real, and it is time to believe survivors. It's time to speak.

Resources

Podcasts
"The Covert Narcissism Podcast"- Renee Swanson
"The Narcissistic Abuse and Recovery Podcast"- Caroline Strawson

Books
The Covert Passive Aggressive Narcissist- Debbie Mirza
The Wizard of Oz and Other Narcissists- Eleanor Payson
Why Is it Always About You- Sandy Hotchkiss
The Human Magnet Syndrome- Ross Rosenberg

TikTok
@npdandme

Websites
covertnarcissism.com
cnglifecoaching.com
selfloverecovery.com
thehotline.org
domesticshelters.org
narcissistabusesupport.com

Phone Number
National Domestic Violence Hotline 1-800-799-SAFE

Glossary of Narcissism

Coercive Control: A form of domestic abuse, or intimate partner violence. It describes a pattern of behaviors a perpetrator uses to gain control and power by eroding a person's autonomy and self-esteem. This can include acts of intimidation, threats, and humiliation. (medicalnewstoday.com)

Cognitive Dissonance: Anxiety or discomfort that results from simultaneously holding contradictory or otherwise incompatible attitudes, beliefs, or the like, such as when someone likes a person but disapproves strongly of one of their habits. (dictionary.com)

C-PTSD: Complex post-traumatic stress disorder can result from experiencing chronic trauma, such as prolonged child abuse or domestic violence. (clevelandclinic.org)

Flying Monkey: A popular psychology term that refers to an enabler of a highly narcissistic person or someone with narcissistic personality disorder (NPD). A flying monkey is an agent who acts on their behalf. (narcissiticabuserehab.com)

Gaslighting: The use of psychological manipulation to undermine a person's faith in their own judgment, memory, or sanity. (dictionary.com)

Grey Rock Method: Deliberately acting unresponsive or unengaged so that an abusive person will lose interest in you.

Hoovering: When someone engages in unhealthy behaviors used to manipulate people back into their lives. (Psychcentral.com)

Love Bombing: The action or practice of lavishing someone with attention or affection, especially in order to influence or manipulate them. (dictionary.com)

Narcissistic Personality Disorder: A personality disorder characterized by extreme self-centeredness and self-absorption, fantasies involving unrealistic goals, an excessive need for attention and admiration, and disturbed interpersonal relationships. Abbreviation: NPD (dictionary.com)

Narcissistic Supply: Anything and anyone that narcissists use to regulate their self-esteem. The purpose of narcissistic supplies is to enhance the narcissist's sense of being special. (psychologytoday.com)

Trauma Bond: Emotional bonds with an individual (and sometimes with a group) that arise from a cyclical pattern of abuse perpetuated by intermittent reinforcement through rewards and punishments. (wikipedia.com)

Word Salad: A type of narcissistic speech that is purposefully confusing. (psychologytoday.com)

Notes

Mia Hanks is originally from a small rural town in Missouri. She graduated from Vanderbilt University in Nashville, Tennessee, and she has two adult children. Mia shares her home with a rescue dog. Bride-Made, A Memoir is her first book.

miajhanksauthor@gmail.com